The Jug-eared Kid

The Jug-eared Kid

Selected Columns
from
The News-Journal
by
John Carter

The News-Journal - Daytona Beach, Florida

Contents

John Carter, 1998

Foreword

This book is not the sort of thing John would have completely approved of. Too much like puttin' on airs.

"I can just see him rolling his eyes at the whole idea," a close friend of his confided to me.

Oh, probably. But after he got used to the idea, I think he'd be quietly proud that so much of the World According to Carter would be rounded up and put inside a cover.

He wrote more than 700 columns for The News-Journal between 1984 and his unexpected death.

Carter's columns overflowed with his enthusiasms — country cooking ("cheap but larrupin" bowls of white beans, and hoecakes, catfish, speckled perch, barbecue, sweet potato pie . . . "too much ain't enough!") yard flamingos ("Florida's only native art form") fishing on the St. Johns and Lake Okeechobee ("Goin' down to Lake Okeydokey") the wonders of local history and the observance of festibles (which are better than festivals.)

His love for the disappearing world of rural Florida was celebrated in all his columns. They cheered native Floridians and charmed newcomers.

"I tend to stay in one spot and thoroughly fish it," he said, not meaning to get all metaphorical or anything.

He could vividly evoke his life as a jug-eared kid growing up in Jacksonville because he was never more than a step removed from being that kid, grinning in wonder at what happened to him last and planning the next prank, the next party, the next road trip.

Rereading these pieces was like hearing him tell all the best old stories again because his speaking voice and his writing voice were one and the same.

John had so much fun that it was easy to overlook his talents as writer. If you didn't actually see him doing it, he made it look easy.

When committing journalism, John would stare down his typewriter like a wrestling opponent.

He'd pinch his cigarette between his thumb and two fingers, take a deep draw like someone about to dive underwater and commence typing. Furiously. Hard. Faster than you'd think two hooked fingers could go.

He'd halt as though he'd bumped into a wall, take another long drag and repeat.

When this process ended, a small stack of paper would be produced. Without a cross-out, without a typo, without a false start. First try.

The rhythm became only a little less pronounced after he stopped smoking and typewriters gave way to computers and the Formica-topped wooden desks were replaced by cubicles.

John had come to newspapering later in life than is usual. Before he showed up in The News-Journal newsroom in 1976, he already had traveled far and done a lot. He joined the Air Force in 1961 and left with the rank of captain in 1968, earning a BA from South Colorado State College along the way. He was press representative for the Baptist General Convention, worked for Dallas Baptist College and managed a Radio Shack.

But it had been his longtime dream to work at a newspaper and once he got the job, he never completely lost the feeling of a kid who had successfully run away with the circus.

— Mark Lane

The Carter Family

Being a fifth-generation Florida native is a mixed blessing. It is our lot in life to be forever divided against ourselves and confused about our past and present.

— *JC*

Odd Couple Left
Wealth of Memories

Henry David Carter of Surrency, Georgia, and Lillian Catherine Geiger Carter of Jacksonville were quite an odd couple. It was quite a mismatch . . . this pairing of a lanky rawboned Georgia farmboy who never advanced past the third grade and a refined, well-mannered judge's daughter whose family could have inspired a Faulknerian novel.

They were my grandparents, and because of circumstances beyond control or imagining, they raised this little jug-eared kid through a Florida childhood of warm memories and answered prayers.

From 1940 on they submerged their identities to the demanding task of whipping me into some semblance of citizenship. Heck, I even named them . . . my baby talk nicknames of "Nonna" and "Deedy" being picked up by every relative and friend.

She even called him "Deedy" and he called her "Nonna," except when she was mad, when she would spit out: "Dave!" When he was teasing her, he would say in a singsong voice that she was "Madame Queen" or "My Gal Sal."

"Nonna" joined a sewing circle and sipped orange pekoe tea. "Deedy" delivered furniture and dipped snuff. "Nonna" peered through Cokebottle thick glasses to read her Bible. "Deedy" used to sneak a pull off the pint of Seagram's 7 he kept in the glove compartment of his pick-up truck.

Even mild oaths prompted "Nonna's" wrath, and "Deedy" suffered

3

the same affliction as President Harry Truman. He never could train himself to say: "Manure."

When "Nonna" would toast pecan halves in butter, Worcestershire sauce and salt, she would call them: "Pi-KAHNS." "Deedy" accented the first syllable, calling them: "PEE-cans."

Much of "Nonna's" time was spent correcting "Deedy's" many sins of grammar and pronunciation. She tried to get him to say "fire" instead of "fahr" and "help" instead of "hope" and, of course, to rid his speech of the dreaded "ain't."

He smoked big cigars and would turn his hat around backwards if a cat ran out in front of his car. She pounced on him with all the zeal of a reformed smoker ("Nonna" smoked Luckies for years until she quit) and the gusto of an evangelist who considered all superstition to be of Satan his se'f.

It was easy to see why I gravitated more and more as ally and co-conspirator with "Deedy" over the years. "Nonna" took me shopping and made me wear clothes which could have been used in "Revenge of the Nerds." "Deedy" took me fishing and let me steer the boat.

"Nonna" used to make me play the piano when she had the Woman's Missionary Union ladies over to pretend that wearing kimonos and drinking tea was a valid contribution to world missions, while "Deedy" bought me a first baseman's mitt.

"Nonna" frowned if my piano practice deteriorated from "Rock of Ages" to Rock 'n Roll, but grandpa only tapped his foot and laughed.

He told me great stories about the days when he was the most famous square dance caller between Blackshear and Hazlehurst and how when he was in the Navy he went on a ship across the Pacific to "Chiner," and "JAPann."

As different as H.D. and Lillian Carter were, it never entered their minds that their marriage was in any way unusual or abnormal. They lived as man and wife for nigh onto 60 years and I don't recall either one of them ever uttering the word "compatible."

I can still remember him tilting his Panama hat back on his head and pinching "Nonna" on the shoulder and saying: "I love my ole gal Sal." "Nonna" would flutter her eyelashes and get downright coquet-tish. "Oh, Dave . . ." she would say.

Grandfather's Education Came outside School

My esteemed grandfather, H.D. Carter, the squire of Surrency, Georgia, was forced to drop out of school at an early age. His father died when he was 12 and he was forced to become the head of his household, taking care of his mother, brothers and sister.

His family was so poor that they never noticed it when the Depression hit. "Mostly, I noticed that other folks had got about as poor as us," he recalled.

H.D. claimed his education stopped with the Third Reader at Surrency's little one-room school, but actually he was one of the smartest people I've ever known. It's just that his grammar and pronunciation were a mite rough.

He said "heerd" for "heard," "neern" for "none," "fahr" for "fire" and "hoped" instead of "helped." And he had a stockpile of homespun sayings that made him sound like a country bumpkin, but made a curious kind of sense.

Like when anyone would inquire: "Dave, how are you doin'?" He would always reply: "Kickin', but not high!" He defined anyone from up north as "Somebody who don't know that grits is groceries."

If my grandmother or anyone else seemed dissatisfied with anything he had done, ole H.D. shrugged off the criticism with: "If'n you don't like my peaches, you don't have to shake my tree."

Sometimes the tree-shaking went on anyway, and my grandpa would be sorely vexed by the attitude and obstinacy of my grandmother. When he wanted her to hush up her constant carping, he complained loudly that she was "plunkin' on the ole one-string harp" and he was tired of hearing it.

He spent much time exhorting me to be a better person. "I want you to be something, son," he would beseech me, usually around report card time.

If my grades were a little below par, he would threaten me with military school. Back then in Jacksonville, Bolles was an all-boys school where the kids had to wear West Point type uniforms. Almost every little jug-eared kid in town feared that someday his parents would be so fed up with his antics that he would be "sent to Bolles."

If not the threat of military school, my grandfather would raise the specter of farm work, or other manual labor.

"Study hard, son. You don't want to end up like I did, looking an ole ugly mule up the ass plowing a field in the hot sun."

Ole H.D. sure had a way with words.

Anytime he wanted me to come help out delivering or refinishing furniture at his store, H.D. would crash through my bedroom door at about 4 a.m. "Git up, son!" he would shout, "Don't let the sun blister yore back!"

Outside it was still pitch dark and crickets were chirping. I'd get dressed in a T-shirt and jeans and pad out to the kitchen, where H.D. already had the coffee made and it was "saucered and blowed."

H.D. had a one-string harp of his own, and it was a tune I heard over the years from him and all of his kin. It was this, that you should never try to be somethin' you ain't. My grandfather would see some country person trying to be sophisticated and scoff: "Humph! She come to town to see the sights and turned out to be one of 'em."

There was a three-step highway to hubris, according to my Georgia relatives. Somebody just a little conceited was criticized as being "too full of hisse'f." Once you got too full of yourself, you graduated to being "too big for your britches."

The worst sin of all, according to H.D. and his fambly, was the dreaded "puttin' on airs."

There is no worse offense than that in the Georgia backwoods.

I'll never forget when one of my cousins moved to the city, married a city girl, and returned home to Georgia for a visit. The country folk took an instant dislike to the new bride, who had her hair piled up on top of her head and wouldn't do dishes because of her long, polished fingernails.

"Airs" there were on that fateful day, and it was a verdict that the poor girl never recovered from, family-wise.

You'll have to take my word for that, and sorry if you don't approve of my assessment of the situation. Looky here, if'n you don't like my peaches, you don't have to shake my tree.

Young John and grandfather, H.D. Carter

Old Grandad

Anytime I hear anyone say: "Now I'm just a country boy, but . . ." I immediately grab for my wallet and hold on tight. The reason I do so is that I was raised by one of these professional country boys who got rich off of competitors who underestimated his intelligence and business skills.

The late H.D. Carter, esteemed proprietor of Carter Furniture Company of Jacksonville for four decades, taught me through his life's example not to take anyone lightly just because he or she was of low birth or income.

Just before he would move in for a big sale, my grandfather would point out that his education had ended early and that the Third Reader was as far as he got. When he was in the Navy, he learned the simple economic theory of lending $20 on Monday to get $25 back on Friday and "living off that 5 percent interest!"

H.D. Carter wasn't one for cash flow charts, computer printouts and such. He had a simple faith that if you tripled the wholesale price on new furniture and drove a ridiculously hard bargain on used appliances that somehow you would come out okay.

My grandad refused to add interest or carrying charges to his credit accounts, not because he was philosophically against such things, but because that would have made his bookkeeping too complicated.

Among his biggest pigeons were casual acquaintances who assumed that just because they knew somebody who owned a furniture store

8

they would get a break on the price. That's about as smart as figuring that you'll get a big break on the price of a car because you go to the same church as the dealer.

If you believe that sort of thing, I have some land I'd like to sell you down in Camp Swampy Estates.

The wholesale house had a special price list which it offered as a service to those retailers who were trapped into bringing a "friend" or distant relative along to select furniture. The price list had a built in markup which was paid to my grandfather after the customer paid the allegedly "wholesale price" in cash.

It wasn't a lot of money, but my grandad always believed every little dollar helps.

I was H.E. Carter's willing accomplice in many of those business adventures, and he often would take a dip of snuff or pull from the bottle of Seagram's 7 he kept in the pickup truck glove compartment and tell me how to come out on the good end of every trade.

By the time I was old enough to help out at the store, he involved me in all phases of the business — collections, refinishing used furniture, inventory, delivery, buying and selling. I went with him to the big furniture market in High Point, North Carolina, and a couple of times I was even trusted to carry the payoff money (styled as a "Christmas present") to the crooked justice of the peace who ruled the district with an iron hand.

Ol' H.D. Carter never got a good education of his own, but he taught me more than I ever learned in any school. He wasn't perfect. He wasn't even close. In fact, he was nothing more than an ingenious collection of rough edges.

But life with my grandad was one swell adventure, and I always felt good when I was around him.

Sometimes I miss Henry David Carter a lot, but when I do it's a curious reaction. I used to feel guilty because I felt an overwhelming urge to laugh when I was supposed to be soberly meditating about him. Now I know it's okay to grin and cry at the same time.

Why Granddaddy Didn't Cotton to Jesup Kin

The bubblegum machine went on . . . and the siren, too. Henry David Carter and I were in the terrible clutches of the Georgia Highway Patrol.

My granddaddy should have known better than to try to go 75 or 80 miles per hour anywhere near Nahunta or Jesup, but it was easy to forget how fast you were moving in those big Buicks of the early 1950s.

The trooper, who was so polite that you could hardly resist the impulse to smash him one in the snoot, invited us to follow him at a respectful rate of speed to the courthouse in Jesup. We did.

The judge, a couple of flunkies and assorted spitters and whittlers were lounging around the room. They perked up when they found out the trooper had brought in a couple of Floridians to fleece. Not as good as New Yorkers or other Yankees, but still potentially lucrative by South Georgia standards.

During the somewhat forced introductions, it was discovered that there was no one in the room — judge, bailiffs, trooper, ne'er do wells, defendant or defendant's grandson — who wasn't related. A couple of them were Carters or close to it, which in those pre-Jimmy Carter days was more of an indictable offense than an honor.

My grandfather could hardly believe his good fortune. He forgot all about the ticket for speeding and relaxed.

He felt like Brer Rabbit in the brier patch. We launched into more than an hour of conversation about such topics as Uncle Elmer and Aunt Mary Lee, about the Groovers and how the Morrises had left the Free Will Baptist Church and formed their own Methodist church a couple of miles down the road.

And about how Miss Birdie sure was a piano ace but couldn't actually read music and only played out of the hymnals with the shaped notes. Or about how Brentwood used to be a bustling little town on the railroad line but had fallen on hard times and now existed only in the memories of Appling and Wayne County oldtimers.

"Umm Dave," the judge interrupted, almost apologetically, "I'd lak to set ahear and tawk with yew all day, but I gotta let the highway pa-TROL-mun git bak to work. So I'm jes' gonna find you twenny five dollahs an' let it go at that."

It took a moment for the $25 fine to sink in. My granddaddy's smile froze, then left his face a twitch at a time. In a tone of voice that would have made Clint Eastwood freeze in his tracks, my gran'pa said: "You sonofabitch. You mean you made me sit here and talk with you for an hour when you were going to fine me anyway? And you call yourself kin?"

H.D. Carter was thin, wiry and perfectly capable of handling himself in an unfair fight. He advanced toward the bench. The judge broke and ran. A couple of bystanders helped me grab my granddad and spare him a major assault and battery charge.

In obvious contempt of court, he pulled a twenty and a five out of his wallet and threw it on the table alongside the ticket that only minutes earlier he was sure he had beaten.

For the rest of his life, my granddaddy told the story about how he had been mistreated by his Jesup relatives and took great satisfaction out of hearing any family gossip that bad fortune had befallen any of them.

Truth was, that H.D. Carter used his status as a family man, veteran, Mason, Baptist Deacon and minor philanthropist with an occasional smidgen of political clout in every way he could to get an edge. It was highly offensive to him that a government agency existed which was impervious to the charms of such an exemplary citizen.

Grandfather's Wisdom
Passed down the Centuries

Saint Thomas Aquinas and H.D. Carter would have gotten along pretty well. Leastways I think they would have.

At first glance, it seems a mismatch. Ole Thomas, born in 1224, studied under Albertus Magnus and the University of Paris and later on became a theological adviser and lecturer to the Pope his own se'f.

He went on to become a big wheel at the University of Naples and a defender of the faith against heretical interlopers.

H.D. Carter, born in 1897, dropped out of the one-room schoolhouse in Surrency, Georgia when he was only 10 or 11 years old. He had only advanced to the Third Reader when his daddy died, and he had to become the head of the household, supporting his mother, sister and brothers.

At an age when Thomas Aquinas was wrestling with Arabian-Aristotelian thought, ole H.D. was looking at the south end of the northbound mule, trying to bring in a meager cotton or sweet potato crop.

About the same time ole Thomas A. was developing scholasticism, H.D. was calling square dances in Baxley and Blackshear.

Saint Thomas may have framed copies of his academic degrees on the wall, but ole H.D. had his degrees in bedrock values such as common sense and thrift.

I think even Saint Thomas would have saluted my grandfather for those admirable qualities.

And after all that time Aquinas spent sitting around chatting with the Pope about theology and all, I'm sure that H.D.'s status as chairman of the deacons at Central Baptist Church in Jacksonville would be a pretty pale experience.

Enough about differences. It's time to get to the good part where Saint Thomas Aquinas and H.D. Carter were firmly in agreement.

The Seven Deadly Sins.

Thomas and H.D. didn't invent the seven deadlies. Textbooks tell us the concept of seven incredibly bad sins goes back to the first Christians huddled in catacombs.

Whatever, there is no debate that these seven traits are pretty doggoned bad, and Saint Thomas Aquinas and H.D. Carter never were shy about saying so.

Aquinas said a deadly sin is morally scrofulous because "it gives rise to others, especially in the manner of a final cause" or motivation.

H.D. pretty much subscribed to the same thought when he would give me parting advice as I would leave the house for a date, or a ball game or to go to school.

He would look up and say: "Don't get into any trouble now, y'hear?"

Here are the seven sins so loathed by Thomas and H.D.: (1) Pride or vainglory (2) Covetousness (3) Lust (4) Envy (5) Gluttony (6) Anger and (7) Sloth.

I have a mixed scorecard on the seven deadlies. Like on No. 7, I am a trifle lazy, else why would I have picked newspapering instead of real work. No. 6? I'm pretty easygoing, but I do get angry at myself sometimes, especially after chili-dipping a chip shot on the 18th green.

Umm, No. 5? Can we skip this one? Okay, yeah, I have a hard time pushing myself away from the dinner table. I'll work on this one.

I do pretty good on 2 and 4 . . . It doesn't bother me much if somebody else hits the Lotto or lives in a bigger house than me. And 3. Uhh, I refuse to answer on the grounds it might incinerate me. I recall even Jimmy Carter had a problem with that one.

Which brings us to Numero Uno and the main area where Saint Thomas and H.D. nod in agreement. Pride is, and ought to be, the worst of the seven deadly sins.

Saint Thomas liked to use high-falutin' words like vaingloriousness,

I guess, or whatever the equivalent is in Latin.

I liked H.D.'s term for it better than the Aquinas version. My grandpa called it "puttin' on airs."

That was the worst thing H.D. Carter could say about anyone, that they were "puttin' on airs." That term described his nephews who went off to Georgia Tech and for a time, until rudely brought back to reality, they forgot where from whence they had come.

My grandpa said: "Son, don't ever try to be someone you aren't and never put on airs."

I promised I wouldn't but then I asked H.D. why every time he bought a new car, he would immediately drive it to Georgia to show off to all his kin.

"That's different," H.D. drawled. "Everybody loves the smell of a new car."

Hmmm. Wonder what ole Saint Thomas Aquinas would have made of that . . .

Lazy Fishing Brings back Old Memories

Getting out on my boat, the venerable S.S. Fort Mudge, on these lazy, hazy days of summer has been a source of rest and introspection for me. When I watch the little pecks of bluegill, red-ear or shell-cracker troubling my bobber as the current brings it to rest near a clump of hyacinth, the memories come flooding in.

They are the swirling memories of my days growing up as a little jug-eared kid in Jacksonville and of my hero-grandfather waking me at 4 a.m. to go on another of our little fishing trips.

"Don't let the sun blister yore back," he would holler as he ripped the covers off my bed and turn on the bright overhead light in my bedroom. Outside, frogs and crickets were chirping and there was not even the faint pink tickle of a sunrise still hours away out my east window.

I slipped on blue jeans, tennis shoes and a T-shirt (sometimes inside out because I was so groggy) and stumbled into our big kitchen, where my grandpa had coffee ready.

Then I was sent to get our old Wizard five-horsepower outboard motor and gas can out of the shed and put it in the back of our pickup truck, while my grandpa rounded up our cane poles, tackle box and ice chest.

Sometimes the destination would be as far south as Lake Lochloosa or Cross Creek, but nine times out of 10 he aimed the truck toward Black Creek, a tributary of the St. Johns River in Clay County.

15

It's hard to believe now that the Doctor's Inlet and Black Creek area are practically suburbs of Jacksonville, but in the 1940s it was a wild and beautiful place. Coffee-colored water meandered under trees draped with moss. Some parts of the creek were so choked with hyacinths that the local fish camp owners went through them each day just to keep boat trails open.

You could spend all day fishing the little twists and turns sometimes without ever running into another person.

My grandpa took these idyllic summer days as opportunities to teach me little life lessons, such as the virtues of baiting your own hook and taking your own fish off and putting them in the live well or on the stringer.

He told me stories about his days on the farm in Georgia, and how times were once so hard that he joined the Navy just so he could send his paycheck, uncashed, home to his momma and his brothers and sister.

He lived off money he made doing chores and taking extra duty details for other sailors while they went on liberty in foreign ports.

As we waited for the fish to bite, ole H.D. Carter would preach thrift and the virtues of getting a good education and about being courageous, standing up for yourself and "being a man."

He talked about the necessity to be loyal to your family and to God, in that order, and how you needed to be a friend if you wanted to have friends, not to look down on any man "jes' because he was pore," and that people judge you by the quality and the shine on your shoes.

He let me take a puff off of his cigar and told me I could even take a pull off the pint of Seagram's 7 he kept in the tackle box as long as I would not tell my straightlaced Baptist grandma what he had done.

Childhood Locale Helps
Decide Big Meal's Name

"Uncle Will" Addison was a curmudgeon who lived down near Lake Okeechobee. He was one of the colorful Floridians interviewed by the great Florida raconteur and historian Al Burt in an anthology titled "Becalmed in the Mullet Lattitude."

In this remarkable interview, Addison bemoaned how times had passed him by and unmanaged growth had caused almost everything he liked to be outlawed. He used to sell egret feathers, hunt alligators, raise cattle near the big lake and fish with entry-long trotlines.

However, the most heinous thing that Uncle Will could think of was this: "They even changed dinner and supper to lunch and dinner," he growled.

That struck a real chord in me, because my family has been split asunder over the years about whether the evening meal was rightly called dinner or supper and whether the midday repast was dinner, supper or lunch.

Don't even mention brunch. Never heard that word till I was growed.

It seems to have some connection with whether you are a city mouse or a country mouse. Farm folk tend to call the evening meal supper and city denizens call it dinner.

When I was just a little jug-eared kid, we called the evening meal dinner because it was the biggest meal of the day. We were pretty much correct dictionary-wise, since that is the definition of dinner.

However, my Georgia kin tended to eat big meals around noon, and then just put a tablecloth over the leftovers to keep the flies off it. Then the cloth was removed for the evening meal, which was called supper.

On Friday I was looking for research tomes on this topic. I was handed a book titled: "1001 Things Everybody Should Know About The South," from which I quote:

"Dinner in the South used to mean the midday meal — the principal meal of the day as in many agricultural societies. The lighter evening meal was supper. But as Southerners have moved to town, the major meal was moved to evening and the name has moved with it, except in many cases on Sunday."

According to a poll cited in the book, 57 percent of Southerners now eat dinner in the evening (That puts me in the majority), while only 40 percent still eat supper then. We don't know what happened to that other 3 percent. I assume they just eat and don't call it anything.

Among non-Southerners, the numbers are 65 percent in favor of dinner.

I guess old-timers and farmers think that's a shame, recalling the old gospel song "Suppertime" and sourly pointing out that Jesus ate a Last Supper and not a Last Dinner.

I reckon they go to Supper Clubs and sing for their supper.

I'm a big fan of Dinner-on-the-Ground and Dinner Theaters and I think most cats perk up their ears when they hear someone calling them for "din-din" but I think they would mostly yawn and lick their paws if you said "sup-sup."

H.D. Carter, my grandpa, used both words interchangeably. That came from being raised on a farm but then living for many years in the city, I guess.

Sometimes he would come through the kitchen door after a hard day at his furniture store and ask "if dinner was ready yet?" Other times he would grin and say, like many country people do, "You can call me anything as long as you call me for supper."

I've kinda got into the habit of calling all meals dinner. That' what's s'posed to be the major meal of the day and doggoned if they all aren't considered major by me.

And I've got the waistline to prove it.

Child's Hero Lives in
Gift from Momma

In this materialistic age, it's sometimes tempting to judge a gift by its price tag, and not by its symbolic nature. Maybe that's because most of us have quit taking the trouble to give gifts fraught with symbolism and take the easy way out.

Anyhow, I'm going to brag on my momma some this morning, because she has a genius for picking out things that are really meaningful. On one of my visits to her home in Broward County a few years ago, Mom brought out a cigar box full of personal effects that had belonged to her dad — my grandfather Pappy Cone.

I hold warm and happy memories in my heart of ole Pappy, who used to call all the young'uns "Smokey" and would take us fishing and tell us neat stories and spend more time with us than he did with the grownups, so naturally he was our favorite.

Momma, in her wisdom, knew that it would be nice to have something tangible to remind me of Pappy's smiling face, so she told me to take my pick from the cigar box. I was immediately attracted to a gold ring, which I slipped on my finger. It fit perfectly, and I've worn it ever since.

Mom's gift-giving skills have not diminished since. Last weekend, she was cleaning up a few things around our cabin at Lake Okeechobee and she asked me if I wanted some of the pictures that have been on the walls there since the early 1950s.

I hesitated to accept at first, because a couple of those pictures are among my mom's greatest treasures and it would be hard for me to explain how much she loves and misses her daddy without getting all mushy and stuff.

But she was serious, and I finally have on my wall at home a photo of Pappy Cone which I have admired since I was a pup and sorta grew up with. It was taken by a longtime family friend, Johnny Walther, who was an ace photographer for the Miami Herald back in those days.

It shows Pappy grinnin' like a possum eatin' briars and holding up a prime example of Lake Okeechobee's bass population. Back in those days, before the flood control dike that now rings the big lake was finished, the preferred method of bass fishing was the way Pappy and his drinking buddy Cleve Barlow did it . . . without a boat.

Pappy and almost all of my relatives on my momma's side would prowl the shallows of Lake O for bass, speckled perch and even a little frog gigging. None of 'em were rich, but they ate good and partied hard.

His skill as a fisherman, storyteller and all around good ole boy became legendary in South Florida. Though he never held public office, owned a company or wrote a book, the Miami Herald gave Pappy more than a quarter of a page obit when he died. With the death notice was this picture, the one that I own now, of Pappy celebrating a big catch.

The obituary was a little syrupy, filled with references to the fact Saint Peter and Pappy probably are getting along well up in heaven because they both were fishermen, but we liked it. A little truth snuck in, such as the admission that one thing he did not have in common with the heavenly gatekeeper is that Pappy was no saint.

He bet the horses and drank a bit. He cussed some, but rarely around the ladies. He was mischievous and acted just like us kids.

It's hard to believe, but I'm now getting to the age that Pappy was when I thought he was just about the greatest old guy in the world. But when I look at his picture on my wall, I feel just like a little jug-eared kid again, and I remember him calling me "Smokey" and teasing me about the girls and the time we really slayed 'em when he took me snook fishing.

It's a gift that keeps on giving. Thanks, Mom.

History Rides in the
Back of a Pickup Truck

I did something t'other day that made me kind of sad.

We had some company from up in Jacksonville, the world's largest village and my home town, and amongst the kids was a 10-year old stumpknocker named Phil.

It didn't take long for the young'uns to conjure up an expedition to the swimming pool and maybe by the store for candy and I was elected to be the chauffeur.

Phil asked if he could ride in the back of my pickup truck and I said no. I kinda wanted to let him and it isn't against the law near as I can tell, but it didn't seem like the safest thing to do.

So he climbed in, buckled up like a good buckaroo, and rode up front with me.

I've thought about that a lot since then, wondering if I shouldn't have let him do it. I know I made the right decision, political-correctness-wise, but I remembered my own days as a little jug-eared kid growing up in Jacksonville and South Georgia when I logged a powerful number of miles in the back of a pickup.

Some of it was work. I delivered furniture for the family business, Carter Furniture Co. ("You want to buy, see us. You want to sell, call us") on Old Kings Road.

The rest of it was fun. There were trips to swimming holes and watermelon patches and sometimes just me and my cocker spaniel "Rusty" who always looked like he was laughing when the wind hit him in the face and flopped back his ears.

The best birthday I ever had was my 10th (or it could have been my 11th.) These days some of the years are starting to telescope on me, you understand) when my grandpa took me and a few other hellions to the Jacksonville Zoo.

We waved and shouted and made faces at passing cars and did all the little things which make boys so doggoned endearing. When the tailgate came down, we ran screaming through the zoo, chasing the peacocks that roamed the grounds and feeding peanuts to the elephant.

The highlight for us and the lowlight for my folks was when we all jumped into Trout River and emerged with our clothes all dripping wet.

It was probably good we were carried home by truck. We would have ruined the upholstery of a car.

I have a buddy, Jerry Jeff. He not only sings about pickup trucks, he tells pretty neat stories about them. My favorite is about the time Jerry Jeff was riding at night in the beautiful Texas Hill Country west of Austin. His co-conspirator was none other than the late great Hondo Crouch, the poet-goat-farmer-curmudgeon who founded the modern incarnation of Luckenbach, population 25, altitude 1,561 feet.

As they crested one of the hills, Hondo cut the engine and turned out the headlights. "Let's go for the coastin' record," he said.

The ribbon of road was illuminated by a Luckenbach Moon, a formidable force about which I will say more shortly.

Hondo opined the current "coastin' record" to be a tree by the side of the road a good piece from the bottom of the hill. That said, he eased his foot off the brake and the truck started rolling.

Jerry Jeff always gets a laugh when he tells how he got caught up in Hondo's little joke and actually was leaning forward in the cab, trying to make the truck go faster.

Hondo Crouch, acknowledged as the Hill Country's "Semi-official Poet-Lariat," once wrote a poem about the Luckenbach Moon. His imagery is something else. My favorite snippets are the part where he says: *"This kind of moonshine makes you crazy if you sleep in it."* And, *"Those who saw the moon said they could smell it. One said it*

22

tasted like sin."

Or, *"A kind of moon that makes haunted houses uglier. And ugly girls prettier."*

Hondo was right on. I've seen that moon my own se'f. One time it was while we were having a few beers sitting on the tailgate of an old pickup truck.

Don't know who wrote this, but some guy once said this about Luckenbach and the Hill Country: *"It's kinda like Brigadoon; you're almost afraid to go back because it might not be there again."*

John and brother Don, Jacksonville, 1946

New Heroes Rekindle
Some Old Memories

The wonderful performance of our firefighters is no surprise to me. It's the kind of magnificent dedication some other professions claim to have, but with the men and women of the fire corps, it's for real.

I hail from a family that boasts several firefighters, and all have served or are serving today with distinction.

My grandmother, Lillian Geiger Carter, was born in Jacksonville in 1901. That's a year that every Jacksonville schoolboy knows brought our "Great Fire."

My grandma had no memories of the fire, of course, but she talked about it often almost as if she had. All the old-timers did.

Her sons, John and Frank, both were scarred by a childhood accident involving fire. So, no one was surprised when both the Carter boys, my dad and my Uncle Frank, ended up on the Jacksonville Fire Department.

My dad eventually went on to other things, but Frank stayed the course. A self-described C-student who had to work hard at school, he applied himself to his work with a passion I've not seen anywhere else.

He came out of the Navy in World War II and took a job on the lowest rung of the fire ladder. He polished brass, washed trucks, folded fire hoses, scrubbed floors and became a pretty good firehouse cook, when it came his turn.

He hustled to thousands of fires during his career. Some were ordinary, like a blaze from one of those cheap "Red Hot" heaters.

Others were complicated and damn near diabolical, such as some of the shipyard fires on the Jacksonville waterfront.

Frank Carter was, and is, serious about the firefighting profession. He worked at it, believed in it.

That's why he hated the politics that affected the fire department so much. His upward mobility through the ranks was slowed at times by his refusal to "play the game" and use political pull.

The most wonderful memory I have of Uncle Frank was him hunched over the dining room table, with books and charts and handwritten notes all around.

When he had his head down, memorizing and rememorizing the command and control structure, the properties of different chemicals in fires, handling of hazardous materials and the specifications of fire suppression equipment, no one could bother him.

I would start to say something to him, but Aunt Betty would remind me: "Y'all be quiet now, Uncle Frank is studying."

I think that is the part about firefighting most people don't know. If the job was a simple matter of brute force, we'd still have the old bucket brigades of antiquity. The cerebral nature of the art and science of fire suppression is rarely discussed, except by those who grew up around firefighters.

Through sheer force of will, Frank Carter forged a 48-year career that took him from the lowest job on the force to deputy chief, the highest post anyone could get without some real juice at City Hall.

At the end of his career, it was his pleasure to coordinate the activities of the many volunteer departments that serve Jacksonville's outlying areas. He developed a strong admiration for the volunteers, who soon became his favorites.

They love firefighting, and to Frank Carter, that's the only qualification that matters.

We see images of our heros wearing yellow protective gear, spraying water on a fire, or helping some family save its home, but in my mind's eye I see all these men and women with heads down at a dining room table, poring over scientific formulas, schematics and thick books . . .

"Y'all don't bother Uncle Frank now, he's studying."

Recalling My Uncle Frank and My Other Uncle Frank

I have two Uncle Franks and both have been a huge factor in my life . . . one early and one late.

Both were born with the name Francis and each went to great lengths to change his name to Frank as soon as possible. Some of the other members of our family still call them Francis once in a while and they have to grin and bear it.

I didn't come from just a broken home. It was shattered. In the aftermath, I ended up as the ward of my grandparents when dear ole Dad hit the road for parts unknown. We later found he had been driving a truck in Kansas City and then found work in a South Chicago steel mill.

My father's brother Frank stepped in to provide some of the nice little touches of my boyhood. He gave me my first baseball glove, took me to the zoo and once let me use his fireman's badge to go through the pass gate at the Gator Bowl game.

There's never been a time when he wasn't available to lend a helping hand or word of encouragement. The lady he married, my lovable Aunt Betty, has been just as dependable and, well, she's a dear.

The other Uncle Frank Cone, my mother's brother, was on the periphery of my growing up years. I saw him only once in a while, and the main memories I had were visiting his Brentwood area house when I was in the second grade in Jacksonville.

Both Uncle Franks have had successful careers, despite what some might say was a lack of major league formal education. The Uncle Frank Carter who helped raise me went from a rookie fireman in 1948 to a deputy chief today.

And I'm proudest of the fact that he did it by studying and working hard and not because he had any political pull at City Hall. I remember the many nights he spent with his head down over textbooks and workbooks at the dining room table getting ready for the promotion exams.

I lost contact with my mom's brother but heard occasional reports about how he had become an expert at turbine engineering and nuclear power plant technology and was working for Westinghouse in Ohio. For years, I only heard about his achievements second hand.

He retired shortly after an assignment to build a nuclear power plant in the Philippines, and as luck would have it, he selected the Lake Okeechobee area where he and my Aunt Dean, bless her heart, too, would set up their new home.

He has such a strong concept of family that Frank and Dean Cone welcomed me wholeheartedly into their home even though for practical purposes we were dern near strangers. Over the past couple of years, we have become best fishing buddies and have caught up for the missing years as we sat in a boat pursuing the wily bass and the prolific speckled perch.

At family gatherings they have hosted, I have come back into contact with other relatives, such as my Uncle Bryan who lived most of his life in Massachusetts but now has retired to Crystal River, and my Uncle Dan and Aunt Ruby whom I saw quite a bit of in Jacksonville but then lost contact when they retired to Lake Wales.

Anyhow, the point of all this is that in your own family you may have someone, a long lost uncle, aunt, nephew, niece or second cousin twice removed who would be thrilled to death if you took the time to make contact. As I bask in the joy of a friendship renewed and feel comforted once more by family ties, I want to certify to you that it's worth the effort.

And I'm being doubly Frank with you about that.

Dance Calling to Bear
Stories, H.D. Was a Talker

When I was but a little jug-eared kid growing up in Jacksonville, my grandpa used to tell me stories. He was a country boy with poor spelling and writing skills, but he compensated for those shortcomings with facile and even eloquent speech.

When he was a young buck growing up in Appling County, Georgia, H.D. Carter gained some fame as a square dance caller. That was no small accomplishment, as a caller with the gift of gab could make a handsome income and meet a lot of girls in those days just before the world war.

World War I, that is.

I don't want to brag, but my granddaddy used to get requests to call square dances from as far away as Blackshear, Waycross and Alma. Ole H.D. used to nudge me and wink conspiratorially and tell me that square dance callers were sort of like lead singers in a rock band . . . they acquired groupies, sort of.

It was always hard of me to imagine my grandfather as some sort of barnyard Lothario or bucolic Mick Jagger, but I took him at his word. I never doubted that all of his claims were true, and nobody else did either. He was of a mind that a man's word was his bond and a firm handshake was all the contract you ever needed to "do bidness" with H.D. Carter.

H.D. grew up in that South Georgia brew of fundamentalist religion, hard farmwork, hot days, cold nights, folktales and superstition.

28

It was a world of making do, of slaughtering a pig an "eatin' everything but the squeal."

Every time we ate chicken, H.D. would wisecrack that when he was young the only piece he got to eat was the "part that goes over the fence last. We was so poor that we even ate the feet and the beak."

He grew up never owning more than one pair of shoes at a time, and that pair was lovingly cared for. "You can always tell a man by his shoes, Son," he would drawl, which was a cryin' shame because shoes and socks are not things real high on my list of priorities.

To young H.D. and his Georgia kin, shoes were important . . . not to be worn for anything other than church or special convocations at school.

Not that school was any place he had much experience with. Ten-year-old H.D. dropped out of Surrency's pitiful little one-room school when his daddy died and he became the head of his household.

He was quite a little man, running the farm and taking good care of his mother and his brothers and sister. When the young'uns would cry for candy, he would pour a little cane syrup in a hot frying pan until it caramelized. When the little ones were fitful and wouldn't go to sleep, he told them stories.

It was about then he created his two most lovable characters — the red bear and the blue bear. And those were the stories that entertained and hypnotized me when he trotted them out again in the early 1940s.

He loved kids and he got a real kick out of telling stories which alternately aggravated and delighted. The red bear/blue bear series was diabolically crafted to do just that.

He would place the two bears in funny situations, usually where they were competing with each other. H.D. was a great checkers player, so sometimes he would end the story with a checkers match, and sometimes the bears would compete for who could catch the most fish at the fishin' hole or who could win a foot race.

Sometimes the red bear and the blue bear would make a bet on who could bust and eat the most watermelons or who could string the most tobacco or lay the most sweet potato vines or pick the most cotton.

Right before the end, H.D. would pause, and then set the hook. "Which one do you want to win?" he would drawl innocently. I don't remember the first few times I ever fell for the bear story scam, but my relatives tell me I liked the color blue and always picked the blue bear.

H.D. would commence at that point to turn the table in favor of that old red bear, giving him some temporary advantage in the competition against his blue brother. At that point, I would scream, objecting to the impending win of the undeserving red bear.

My grandpa then would smile and figure out some Rube Goldberg twist of the tale that would allow the blue bear to snatch victory from the jaws of defeat. Relieved and happy, I then padded off in my little jammies with feet in them to bed, which was the goal all along.

I have a grandson now, and he's starting to scoot around and say a few words. I don't think it's gonna be too long now before little Conner will want me to tell him stories.

I'll put him in my lap and commence . . . Let's see now. There was a red bear and a blue bear, and one day they sat down to play checkers . . .

John at five years.

Lazy People Can Blame Their Genes

A while back we discussed the seven deadly sins, which are, in case you forgot: Pride, Envy, Gluttony, Lust, Wrath, Covetousness and Sloth.

And that column was based on how Pride was first on the list, and deservedly so, but there is big news on the deadly sin front and I wanted you to be among the first to know about it.

There has been a major finding concerning Sloth, and it raises some interesting questions about laziness in general.

Professor Susan Ward, director of the Center for Exercise Science & Medicine at the University of Glasgow in bonnie Scotland, says her research team has discovered a link between laziness and genetics. That's a finding that explains a lot in my family.

It makes sense to me.

Sloths, the animal kind, are slow moving and hang upside down in trees. There's a whole bunch of sloths hanging upside down in the Carter family tree, and I feel the stirring of those genes in my own weary bones.

A genetic link to laziness is a "feel-good" theory for me, because it absolves me of my various procrastinations and screw-ups and places the blame squarely where it belongs — on someone else!

My ancestors made me not do it.

Let's let the good professor explain.

"People who don't like exercise are usually seen as lazy, but it may

31

be that it's not their fault," she told the London Telegraph last week. "There may be a link between exercise intolerance and genetic make-up which restricts or promotes exercise depending on your genes."

Damn! I like that. "Exercise intolerance." My symptoms exactly. I really love the sound of that phrase. Exercise intolerance . . . Exercise intolerance . . . Exercise intolerance. It kind of rolls trippingly off the tongue.

Anyhow, the prof goes on: "If we can establish a certain genetic pattern which corresponds to what is commonly seen as laziness, it could transform the way we deal with health problems caused through lack of exercise."

I can see it now. We already have facilities like the Betty Ford Clinic for substance abuse and such. I foresee the day when we will have a "John Carter Clinic," which will attract lazy people from around the world for self-esteem boosting and reassurance that it's not their fault.

I have begun work on my new book establishing a treatment regimen. The title is "I'm OK. You're So-So."

I think the clinic ought to be in the Greater Daytona Beach Area, not just because this is where I live, but because we are the home of the giant ground sloth and even have his lazy bones on display at our museum.

Forget that World's Famous Beach stuff. We can be the Sloth Capital of the World!

You may not know this, but fruit flies have many genes in common with humans. (I'm not making this up.) Two mutant strains of the little critters have been studied by the Glasgow team, one of which was genetically predisposed to "sitting," while another, dubbed the "rover" strain, was more active.

Not many rover genes around my house. The Carter coat of arms is emblazoned with a motto which translates: "Sometimes I sit and think, and sometimes I just sit."

Stay tuned. I'm continuing work on my book and the clinic. And I'll finish those projects someday. Tomorrow?

Right now, it's nap time, and I feel another genetic attack of slothfulness coming on.

Giving 'Slim'
the Credit He Deserved

His name was Edwin Eather Carter, but we all called him "Slim." He was not a well-known person; in fact this is the first time his name ever has appeared in a newspaper. I don't believe there was even an obituary printed after he died.

And some members of my family, especially the older kin of my late grandpa, may be offended by putting so much information about our family right out where everybody can see it.

But I'll have to take that chance, because I want to make a serious point about compassion, and how our society is judged by the way we treat the least of our brethern.

Slim was my granddaddy's younger brother, and he lived in our home almost the whole time I was growing up, except for the last few years, which is a main part of the story.

Back when I was a kid of about 11 or 12 years old, I played a role in the liberation of Slim. I sorta freed him from the stereotypes and the prejudices that some people had about him.

E.E. Carter was tongue-tied. He was born that way, and everyone in his country family and the neighbors in the Surrency-Baxley area of Georgia thought Slim was retarded.

He was not allowed to go to school because "hit twarn't enny use," as my Georgia kin would say. He was put to hard farm work, but in that sense he wasn't as much the victim of bias as he was of the Depression and the Calvinist work ethic of his peers.

33

Slim lived a life of curious paradox, in which he was alternately treated as if he were a dumb daft animal and as a fragile, afflicted child. Children teased him unmercifully, in that way which seems so cruel to us today but was a way of rural life in rural hardscrabble times.

While Slim lived with my grandparents and me at our 10th Street home in Jacksonville, he was a general handyman at the new/used furniture store which was the fount of our livelihood.

I was the only one who was truly happy-go-lucky and irresponsible, so I was the only one who had enough time to reflect on the nature of things and society in general.

Questions occurred to me at age 11 and 12 like: If Slim is supposed to be so dumb, why does he always make sure he gets the correct change when he buys an RC Cola and a moon pie at the corner grocery? And I also wondered: Why does Slim always laugh at exactly the right places at the cartoons and also at Gabby Hayes and Smiley Burnette in the western shown at the Capitol Theater every Saturday? And: Why is he such a safe and reliable driver, and knows so much about repairing cars?

I kept asking fool-kid questions like that until my folks, who loved me dearly, treated me with respect and cared about what I said even when I was a child, started wondering the same things.

In various family conferences and discussions that followed, the Carters came to a startling conclusion for an Ozzie and Harriet type family of the '50s. Slim had a speech impediment. He wasn't a dummy.

As the family began treating him with more respect and trusting him with ever more complex tasks and concepts, Slim continued to grow and thrive. It wasn't long before he drove off in his shiny, gray car and moved into a small farmhouse in Georgia, where he lived happily ever after in dignity.

We don't always give people enough credit. And I wanted to say that today, somehow, even if my folks get a little put out at me for talking about southern-fried family secrets in front of strangers.

Everybody has a right to be somebody. No matter what race. No matter what handicap. No matter what upbringing.

No matter what.

Palmphleteers Make a Splash with Mullet

The third Tuesday of every month, Brother Ralph Phelps and Brother H.D. Carter would take off work a little early and start intense preparations for the Men's Brotherhood Fish Fry over to the Central Baptist Church parking lot.

Brother H.D. Carter's furniture store was just down Broad Street from Heeth Brothers Seafood Company and he had a pickup truck, so he would recruit me, his ever faithful grandson and co-conspirator, to run by Heeth's to pick up a barrel of scaled, cleaned and split mullet.

By the time we arrived at the parking lot at Central Baptist, Brother Ralph Phelps already would have his apron on and would be bringing the big fry baskets, huge pots and gallon cans of shortening out to the brick pit where a fire was just starting to get right.

My job was to mix up a tubful of batter and drop mullet into it, then fish them out and drop them into the hot grease. Brother Ralph Phelps looked after the cookin' fish, not dipping them out until they suited his rigorous standards for doneness.

By this time, Brother Willie Chitwood would drive up with huge pans of cole slaw and baked beans in back. He would holler over to some of the kids playing touch football next to the railroad tracks and make them haul the brimming containers of slaw and beans to the picnic table which served as our informal buffet.

The crowd eventually grew to about 200 Brotherhood stalwarts, who stood there talking about hunting, fishing, and whether the red thermometer sign next to the parking lot was accurately reflecting the current percentage of money raised for the big church building fund. Seemed like the fishing and hunting never were as good as they used to be and the thermometer sign was hopelessly out of date, because Brother Robert Witty, our beloved pastor, said so.

Every once in a while, some malcontent would register a protest of sorts and ask why we didn't feature a fancier entree for the monthly fish fry, whereupon Brother H.D. Carter would look up, drawl a mild barnyard oath and ask: "Whut's wrong with mullet?"

I was grown before I ever knew anyone didn't like mullet, or that it would become what state officials call an "underutilized species."

Hell, I can't remember the Carter family out of Jacksonville ever underutilizing this abundant species. And neither did that bunch of Wilders over to Port St. Joe, who all grew up munching on mullet as their fish-fry fare of choice.

So it's a good thing that Todd Wilder, a development representative with the state Department of Natural Resources, is on duty as our designated Florida native to spread the word about the noble qualities of this underutilized blessing.

Todd's office is the one responsible for a neat series of brochures the Bureau of Marketing and Extension Services distributes.

One of those slick little pamphlets is dedicated to mullet.

Todd told me the mullet harvest for 1985 was 19.3 million pounds, which may sound like a lot, but isn't nearly enough. A lot of the catch is consumed in Florida, but there are significant out-of-state markets in places such as Detroit and Los Angeles.

Personally, I think that if this noble native resource is ever to escape the underutilized tag, it will be smoked mullet that leads the way. I suggest substituting the smoked variety in the party dip.

To discover the true flavor of Florida life, hit the brakes next time you see one of those crude roadside hand-lettered signs that offer smoked mullet for sale.

If you want to see Florida like a native, or if you even dream of someday being made an honorary Floridian, then you've got to shuck some of your prejudices against those "underutilized species."

Eatin' and Singin' Sure Goes Good with Preachin'

Memorial Baptist Church, a few miles south and west of the Georgia hamlet of Surrency, is not an imposing cathedral. I haven't seen it lately, but in my childhood the church was a small, white frame building sitting up on blocks on a red clay road.

Across the road, decorated with faded, dead flowers and fluttering ribbons were a few graves of the prayer warriors who had gone before. Some of my distant kin are there, and I feel strangely close to them even though I never knew them.

The congregation was of a particular off brand of Baptist called Free Will. The main difference between the Surrency church and the ones affiliated with the multi-million member and dollar Southern Baptists is that my Georgia relatives didn't believe in the venerable doctrine of "Once Saved, Always Saved."

My Uncle David Mann, a faithful deacon and stalwart of Memorial Church, is more at home with the beliefs of Cotton Mather than Billy Graham. The vision of a frail man clinging to a spider web dangling over the fires of hell was a common one conjured up by the Bible thumping preacher boys who came and went from Memorial.

The number of sermons on God's wrath outnumbered those on his love by a ratio of about 50 to 1. The preachin' and testifyin' was a little strong for those like me who had been tenderized by city life, but it suited my Uncle David, Aunt Dovie and cousins Dink, Herman, Babe, Robert and Shirley just fine.

But there were two things the city and country mice always agreed on — the music and the food.

Miss Birdie was the church piano ace, and she was something to see. She was a stylish stout who put on quite a show as she pounded out gospel songs. Miss Birdie didn't actually read music and over the years, she developed that left hand "walking bass" that most of us recognize as the foundation for 1950s style rock 'n' roll.

On special occasions, visiting gospel quartets made up of earnest and clean cut young fellers would perform — emulating their heroes such as the Blackwood Brothers, the Statlers, the Kingsmen and the Jordanaires of Elvis Presley fame.

It was toe tapping time, and we all enjoyed it immensely. I still do. On my last visit to the Possum Festival up in the Florida Panhandle, my friends had to tear me away from the gospel singing tent.

I've saved the best part for last. If we were lucky, our visit to our farm kin coincided with one of the regular "Dinners on the Ground" at Memorial. There would be all day preachin' and singin' plus the most amazing display of good food on this green earth.

Table after table would groan under the weight of fried chicken, country fried steak, roast pork, fried squirrel and quail with raised gravy, massive earthenware bowls of chicken and dumplings, about 30 different kinds of potato salad, all kinds of homemade pickles, relishes (we always liked a corn and onion concoction they called chow-chow), baked beans with hefty chunks of slab bacon or salt pork swimming on top, biscuits, cornbread (baked and fried), greens — collards, mustards and turnip — rutabagas, baked sweet potatoes, crowder peas, cream peas, snap beans, speckled butter beans, well, I could go on, but I want to leave room in this column for dessert.

White cake with chocolate icing. Devil's Food cake with chocolate icing. Yellow cake with swirls of chocolate running through it. Fresh peach ice cream churned the old fashioned way with the young'uns taking turns at the crank (Seemed like it took forever before it was ready!). Custard pie. Thick apple pie with slices of cheddar cheese on top. Pumpkin and sweet potato pie, wild blackberry cobbler with a thick crust that was soggy and dripping with berry juice.

Off to one side, watermelons chilled in a row of washtubs filled with ice. The shrewd old-timers who sliced the juicy watermelons, which also included some of the tasty "yaller meat" melons a lot of Georgia Crackers favor, always saved that course for last.

They knew from experience that the kids wouldn't be able to resist the chance to hold watermelon seed-spitting contests and that the party would eventually erupt into a full-scale watermelon fight.

Grim-faced mommas would grab their watermelon-juice-soaked young'uns by the ear and march them over to the pickup trucks and head for home. Another Dinner on the Ground at Memorial Church was officially over.

When Radio Brought Folks Together

It was a touching scene. My grandfather would be sitting in an easy chair, reading the Jacksonville Journal and dipping Buttercup snuff. My grandma would be crocheting another doily for the living room to go with the 40 or 50 we already had.

The little jug-eared kid (that's me) would be lying on his stomach on the den carpet, not staying in the lines and creating blue owls, purple apples and red horses in my coloring book.

In the center was a huge piece of furniture, larger than most portable television sets. It had a lighted dial, with ornate wood carvings partly covering a dull brown grille cloth. Pay close attention now young'uns, because this is where it gets near unbelievable. This monster appliance was a radio.

And it was the entertainment center of the Carter family in the 1940s. Television was something some Yankees were fiddling with, but not fated to hit Jacksonville until the very tail end of the decade, October of 1949.

It was possible then for a radio jingle or signature line of a radio production to capture the public imagination in the same way that "Where's the Beef" or "Go ahead, make my day" became modern day watchwords.

I remember the cheery whistle of "Rinso White. Rinso Bright" (tweet-tweet TWEET!), the ominous Squuawwwkkkk! creaking door of The Inner Sanctum and the stirring "Who knows what evil lurks in the hearts of men? The Shadow knows."

My imaginary radio playmates were Henry Aldrich, The Great Gildersleeve, Fibber McGee and Molly, Gangbusters, The FBI At Peace And War, Burns and Allen, The Green Hornet, Jack Benny, Fred Allen, Edgar Bergen and Charlie McCarthy and Mr. Keen, Tracer of Lost Persons. (Or was it Mr. Lost, Tracer of Keen Persons? I forget.) My grandfather and I were faithful buckaroos for Brace Beemer's radio version of The Lone Ranger long before we began to watch Clayton Moore's television portrayal of the masked rider of the plains.

I thought soap operas were icky, but the names and theme songs of most of them seeped into my little skull through osmosis. The womenfolk in my early life were faithful listeners to One Man's Family, Stella Dallas and Our Gal Sunday, the show which asked if a girl from the small mining town of Silver Creek, Colorado, could find happiness as the wife of one of England's most wealthy and titled lords?

Today's radio is limited mainly to endless hours of not very good music and some very dreary talk shows. Every once in a while, some station attempts to bring back one of the great old dramas or comedy shows, but there doesn't seem to be a big market for radio nostalgia even in these days of uncommon interest in trivial pursuits.

But those wonderful old shows are more to me than answers to trivia questions. They were sources of fun and wonderment in an era when our senses weren't pounded to death by the tidal wave of competing interests and entertainment options.

Think it over. Which of today's entertainment offerings is attractive enough to bring your whole family together at 8 p.m. any weekday for nothing more than a quiet evening at home?

Guy Lombardo, Inspector Hearthstone, Amos 'n Andy and the Army-Navy Game could do that in their day. MTV, Miami Vice, The Jeffersons and even The Super Bowl never have. And they never will.

A Sad Farewell
to Mom's Best Friend

No way would I ever try to steal any thunder from our own Aunt Mary and her excellent "Pet Talk" column, but this morning's offering is about a little dog.

Not just any pooch, but a coal-black, tiny little poodle, the type of dog I wrongly assumed I could never love because I always envisioned myself as more the spaniel type.

"Bridget" was her name and she belonged to my mom, who for reasons I don't understand lives in the belly of the Broward County growth monster, down Hollywood way.

It's tough to write the words "was" and "belonged," past tense, because Momma just broke the news to me during a Friday night call that little "Bridget" — blind, often losing her balance and falling face-first into her water dish and with an assortment of kidney and other internal problems — is dead.

She was 19, and it doesn't help much to be told that 19 is a long time in dog-years.

After I hung up the phone, it occurred to me that "Bridget" is a symbol of what has become the golden age in terms of my relationship with my mom. My childhood years with her were disjointed and out of focus because of my parents' divorce, then my early adulthood was disrupted by the U.S. Air Force, which decided the national security depended on my presence in Washington State, Colorado and Greenland.

It was only after I returned to Florida for good that our relationship, and my contact with all my really neat aunts, uncles and cousins on her side of the family, grew into all that it could and should be. And that bouncy, feisty little poodle "Bridget" was right there in the middle of all of it.

It was sort of a family joke that Mom loved "Bridget" more than anyone. And everyone agreed "Bridget" was spoiled rotten.

The dog had all of us trained and she was smarter than we were. One day, she decided she wanted two "cookies" (the rest of the world calls them dog biscuits) instead of one. "Bridget" got her way.

A neighbor once made the mistake of breaking one of the "cookies" into bite-sized pieces and hand-feeding them to "Bridget." From then on, that was the only way she would accept them.

"Bridget" had a favorite blanket and a toy box with 50 little squeeze toys in it, ranging from such favorites as a bright orange rubber carrot to a small blue squeaky lamb. She would poke her nose around the toy box for 30 minutes sometimes until she found the one she wanted.

But the most spoiled rottenest thing of all was that my mom let "Bridget" walk all the the eggshell-colored sectional sofa in the living room. My brother Danny and I were forbidden to sit on that sofa, and I don't remember anyone ever using it, because all socializing was mainly done in the airy Florida room.

I was only half-joking a few years ago when I pronounced that sectional sofa as "untouched by human butt." When they were little my nephews Danny and Donny innocently called it "the picture-taking couch," because the only time they could ever sit on it without getting spanked was when they were being photographed.

Well, "Bridget" had the run of "the picture-taking couch" and almost wore out one spot near the window where she could see who was coming to the door and bark at the postman. My momma just smiled.

Everyone in the family was worried how my mom would handle it when the time came for "Bridget" to go to Doggie Heaven. We shouldn't have worried. She was sad, but philosophical. "It was time," she said softly.

"Bridget" was much loved by her veterinarian and the groomer who

43

clipped her and sent her home so many times with perky pink ribbons tied to her ears. The vet, who had the heart-wrenching job of putting "Bridget" to sleep, even sent my Mom a bouquet of flowers.

"They were so nice," Mom said Friday night, "right in the middle there was this one beautiful, perfect rose . . ."

Pappy Cone with the bass he caught in Lake Okeechobee.
(see page 19)

Old Florida

. . . there are limits to everything.
There is no lake or even an ocean that cannot be fished out
and no animal that can't someday make the endangered list
. . . including us.

— JC

Listen up, Learn about Florida Stuff

After you finish reading this little crash course in Floridana you will be able to pose as a native at any fish fry or barn dance as long as you don't slip up and say "youse guys" instead of "y'all."

Now some of you who don't know that grits are groceries already know that the official state motto is the "Sunshine State." But actually, that slogan hasn't been official for a long time, being adopted by our state lawmakers in 1970.

When I was a young'un, the license plates carried the slogan: "Keep Florida Green," which a lot of us figured was a plea for the damyankees to bring more money. Mention that, and folks will think you've been here for quite a spell.

The state song is of earlier vintage. In 1935, we adopted "Old Folks at Home" by Stephen Foster, even though Foster was a damyankee who picked out the Suwannee River on a map and thought it would sound good in a song.

I know that some of you think the mosquito is our state bird, but "To Kill a Mockingbird" isn't just a book title around these parts. Leave ole Mr. Mockingbird alone because he has been our state warbler since 19 and 27.

Most of you by now have seen a state flag, but if you want to impress anyone, tell them you know the design gradually evolved between 1861 and 1900 when the present flag was adopted by voters in a referendum. However, some Florida natives aren't aware that the first state flag was flown at the inauguration of our first governor, William D. Moseley, in 1845. It had five horizontal bars of blue, orange, red, white and green and boasted the legend: "Let Us Alone."

We could use a flag like that today. Might help us stem the tide of growth management.

The orange blossom, of course, is our state flower and has been since 1909. But few know that the 1967 Legislature, in a spirit of overweening boosterism made "the juice obtained from mature oranges of the species Citrus simensus and hybrids is hereby adopted as the official state beverage of Florida."

The orange tree, however, never made the list of officials. Our state tree, so designated in 1953, is the sabal palm, also called the sabal palmetto.

We have a state animal (the Florida Panther, 1982) two state mammals (the manatee and the dolphin were co-honored in 1975) and two state fish (the largemouth bass taking freshwater honors and the Atlantic sailfish the saltwater title, also in 1975.)

Look smug and brag that no other state has two official fish and the gang will think you've been a Florida Cracker since Andrew Jackson was a pup.

We also boast two state gems. The moonstone was chosen in 1970 in honor of the space industry at Cape Canaveral. (Hint: Florida natives never call it Cape Kennedy.) Agatized coral, a more logical choice, was selected as co-gem in 1979.

After all that, if anyone doubts your Florida heritage, blow them away with a few well-chosen words about Pleuroplaca giganta. It's also known as the horse conch and it's a vibrant pinkish-orange. Since 1969, you know, it's been our state shell.

Edmund Skellings of Dania. That's the answer to a trivia question which goes: "Who was named Florida's poet laureate in 1980?"

I'm pushing Volusia County's legislative delegation to have Sunday Punch named the official state column of Florida. Where else could you learn that "Glenn Glitter," mascot and trademark of the Florida Federation of Garden Clubs, was picked in 1978 to be the state's official litter control symbol?

I ought to charge extra for good stuff like this. . . .

Troubled Waters
Hit Old Bridge

In 18th century Europe, landscaping was done on a grand scale not often seen today. Hills were moved, creeks were damned and trees were shaped so that the lord of the manor would have a perfectly balanced view from his library window or from his second floor balcony.

The most noted proponent of this style was a Northumberland gardener named Lancelot Brown. He had a habit of telling potential clients that their properties had excellent "capabilities."

That word stuck and he is listed in the history books as "Capability Brown."

His capabilities are still on display today at such magnificent estates as Blenheim, Kew, Stowe and Warwick Castle.

There is a place in Florida where the view is so balanced and so charming that I believe it rivals those concocted by "Capability Brown." Anyone can see it, and it's free.

Driving from Anastasia Island to the Ancient City of St. Augustine over the beautiful Bridge of Lions has always been a pleasant and mind-bending experience for me. With the Castillo de San Marcos and its forbidding gray on the right and a skyline dotted with red-tiled roofs and church spires, you can imagine yourself crossing a bridge in Italy or Spain.

It pains me to say this, but my favorite bridge is in danger.

It's on a Department of Transportation hit list to be replaced or restored in the years 2000-2001. Not that this fifth generation

49

Floridian has any illusions that his opinion carries any weight, here is one tiny vote for restoration.

I can't believe anyone would be so heartless and devoid of spirit as to put one of those sterile high-rise spans in its place.

Transportation officials and the Coast Guard report that the bridge is punch drunk from too many hits from barges and the years have caused other structural problems.

The hard heads in the hard hats want a wider channel 'neath the bridge, a requirement which militates against a restoration program.

I think something should be worked out, but time is short. The bridge was named last week as one of 11 "most endangered historic places" in America by the National Trust for Historic Preservation.

There are no guarantees, but a Florida DOT administrator has conceded that mention of the "11 most endangered" status would be placed in any environmental impact statement prepared by the state.

We are indebted to Roy Hunt, a law professor at the University of Florida, for nominating the bridge to that list. Hunt calls it a gateway to the city, offering views which can't be replicated.

The "Capability Brown" for the Bridge of Lions was architect J.E. Greiner. The 1,883-foot bridge was built in 1926, has four towers and two distinctive marble lions.

It was intentionally given a style known as "Mediterranean revival" to complement the surrounding landscape. Its importance to the image of the nation's oldest city was underscored by its inclusion on the National Register for Historic Places in 1982.

But as those of you who loved the old Ormond Hotel can attest, mere inclusion of a historic treasure on that list doesn't guarantee its survival.

Maybe we can't stop progress, but here's hoping we can shape it.

Country Roads Still Show
You the Old Florida

They're more that just brick, asphalt, concrete or two sand ruts through palmetto scrub. Roads are romantic.

About the only road I can't stand is a toll road, and before any of you bother to write or call, yes, darn it, I know that all roads are toll roads in a way. Everybody pays, one way or the other.

Anyhow, to all of you out there who have always believed my true calling was to be a truck driver and not a newsman: This one's for you. Driving and gawking along our roadways has always been one of my prime entertainments.

I still get letters and phone calls on a story I wrote years ago about the nifty old red brick road that runs from Espanola to Hastings. I love that stretch of bumpy, narrow road because you can really get the feel of what it was like to be driving through Florida back in the 1920s. I bet it didn't look a lot different then.

I enjoy driving and can even find something good to say about an interstate, though they aren't even close to being a favorite. Up in Georgia, there are red clay roads such as the ones we used to travel to go to Memorial Free Will Baptist Church near Surrency.

The route took us over one of those scary bridges with no railings and boards missing. They creaked and groaned all the time. You can't really say you've learned to drive until you can drive across those country bridges without any increase in your pulse rate.

The best thing about that old clay road is that it ran past an inter-

51

section that featured a gas station and general store run by Miss Birdie, the piano ace of Memorial Church.

I loved Miss Birdie because she always gave me a cold Nehi grape or strawberry and let me play the old pinball machine, which was illegal for me to play at my early age, and punch out little scrolls of paper on her punchboards, which were illegal gambling devices no matter what age you were.

We are blessed here in our circulation area with a wonderful stretch of highway that is Pure Florida, if you have been away from the North and living down here long enough to appreciate subtlety (the appreciation of which is now the only way to tell a rebel from a damyankee, all other comparisons having given way to growth management.)

For a quick and fun drive that gives you an excellent feel for the place we live take none other than State Road 11, which some of you look at only as a shortcut from Bunnell to DeLand, or DeLand to Bunnell if you want to look at it that way.

Back in the early 1960s when I was an Airman Last Class at McCoy Air Force Base in Orlando, I drove State Road 11 both ways almost every weekend while running home to Jacksonville, where a young man could still take a date to the Phillips Highway Drive-In on Saturday night while his grandmother faithfully washed and dried the duffel bag full of the laundry he brought home.

Even in those near-perfect days, I was impressed by the drive along S.R. 11. It seems that almost every type of Florida landscape is there, except of course for typical Everglades scenery.

I always enjoyed the mile or two where it seemed the Florida landscape was magically transformed from pine trees to palms, right outside your car window. And even in those days there was a great little country store at Cody's Corner, which was a landmark and useful for helping figure how much longer you had to drive to get to either U.S. 1 or to Highway 17.

Another helpful hint: Cody's Corner turnoff is the neat way to drive over to Seville and then go north to Palatka or anything like that. You're not going to live in Florida without ever once going to Palatka, are you?

I'm not recommending that anyone drive all the way from

Jacksonville to Orlando the old way before the days of I-95 and I-4, because the 17-92 way through Casselberry into O-Town has been victimized by growth management to the point it would be hard on your radiator and your temperament.

But even today, anybody who wanted to could leave I-95, run State Road 11 and get back on I-4 without losing time or sanity.

Florida is still out there if you know where to look for it. Stay tuned.

This Cracker Honors
Origin of the Term

"He warn't a-sendin' his young'uns to no teacher that learnt 'em to spell 'taters with a p."

(A turn of the century Cracker explains why a neighbor yanked his kids out of school: From the Florida State Archives.)

We may be on the verge of a breakthrough, folks. A Daytona Beach historian may have found the answer to a question that has bedeviled Floridians for decades.

What is the origin of the term "Florida Cracker?"

I didn't even know the answer to that question and I am one. I am descended from tried and true Cracker stock on both sides of my family. What else could result from the union of a Jacksonville dad and a Palatka momma?

Dana Ste. Claire, curator of history and science for the Museum of Arts and Sciences in Daytona Beach, wrote the storyboards for the current exhibit, "Cracker Culture in Florida History" which went on display last June and won't be dismantled until January.

By Christmas, Dana hopes to publish a book he is putting together based on the data he gathered while creating the exhibit.

"What cracker is this same that deafes our eares with this abundance of superfluous breath?"

(William Shakespheare in "King John," 1594.)

The above quote by Willie Shakespeare his own se'f is Exhibit A in Dana's contention that Cracker was used as early as 1509 in England

54

and had become common enough that it appeared in literature a few years later.

The importance of this and other finds is that Dana confidently explodes the myth the term came from the cracking sound of whips used by poor migrants coming to Florida in the colonial period.

"I should explain to your Lordship what is meant by Crackers, a name they have got from being great boasters; they are a lawless set of rascals on the frontiers."

(Letter to the Earl of Dartmouth, 1766.)

"These Crackers are nomadic like Arabs and are distinguished from savages only in their color, language and superiority of their depraved cunning and untrustworthiness."

(Manuel de Zespedes, governor of Spanish East Florida, in a 1790 letter.)

So much for the whip cracking theory. These dispatches bolster Dana's theory that the origin has something to do with vainglorious boasting and overweening pride. But those Shakespearean gibes and the 18th century criticisms were mild compared to the storm of vilification that rained upon my unillustrious Florida Cracker forebears in the 19th century. Here are some samples:

"The volunteers are called Crackers and as a general thing they are a very corrupt set of men. They drink, gamble and swear and do all manner of discreditable things, and are not withal very good soldiers."

(Dispatch from Lt. Oliver Howard during the Third Seminole War.)

"Stupid and shiftless, yet sly and vindictive, they are a block in the pathway of civilization, settlement and enterprise wherever they exist."

(George Barbour, a visitor from New England, 1882.)

"Crackers make the most unsuitable house you can imagine. I knew a tree to fall on one and beat it right down to the ground — cupboard, crockery and all. A family would be more safe in the crust of a pumpkin and about as well sheltered from the weather as a hen coop."

(Ellen Brown, who moved to Florida from New York, 1839.)

It's pretty obvious that Crackers and Yankees have held a low regard for each other for a long time. I remember my grandmother disliked northerners so much she would refuse to help one who stopped and asked for directions.

Life Springs up along
Banks of the River of Dreams

The Timucuan Indians called it "Welaka," or "River of Waters."

In the early 1500s, Spanish sailors dubbed it "Rio de Corrientes," or "River of Currents," and in 1562 a group of Frenchmen named it "Riviere de Mai," to honor the month of May when they started a settlement on its banks.

Spanish soldiers slaughtered the French three years later and chose the name "San Mateo," the saint whose feast day followed the day the river was recaptured. A mission called "San Juan de Puerto" was built near the river's mouth, and the translation "St. John" was applied by the English and remained over the years through Confederate and U.S. possession of this important waterway.

Sandra Frederick, a writer in our Accent Department here at the Little Miracle of Sixth Street, wrote a wonderful feature on the St. Johns in the last Tuesday's News-Journal, and it got me to thinking about how important it has been in my life.

It has been a source of entertainment, food, transportation and, the most important part, incredible beauty, for most of my 58 years. It is my unshakable belief that there is nothing anywhere near like it, anywhere in the world.

For the record, the St. Johns is one of the longest rivers in the world — 310 miles. It is more than two miles wide in some places between Jacksonville, where my daddy was born, and Palatka, my momma's birthplace.

Down this way, where it is narrower, it suddenly widens into large lakes — Winder, Poinsett, Harney, Jesup, Monroe and George — and offers easy access to such treasures as Crescent Lake and Dead Lake in Putnam and Flagler counties and our own Lakes Dexter and Woodruff in Volusia.

It's my favorite river, I reckon, because it is such a lazy river. The total drop from its source in the swamps down near Lake Hell n' Blazes southwest of Melbourne to its mouth at Mayport is less than 30 feet.

It's one of the few U.S. rivers which flows north, but the tidal action from Mayport during periods of low water can cause a reverse flow (old-timers say "the river's runnin' backwards") for 160 miles, as far south as Lake Monroe.

That's good for folks paddling canoes, but bad for the river's ability to flush urban and agricultural runoff out of its system.

I was born in Jacksonville, a place dominated by the St. Johns River since its founding as "Cow Ford," a spot where livestock could swim or be ferried across. At various times, I lived on both the north and south sides of the St. Johns, and well remember childhood fishing trips to the bridges along Hecksher Drive, where my grandfather and I caught croakers for the dinner table and threw back the hated toad-fish which so often stole your bait.

It was a boy's dream come true when my folks bought a house on Big Pottsburg Creek, a tributary of the big river, and a 16-foot run-about with a motor big enough we could use it for water-skiing.

After high school, I enrolled at Jacksonville University. At a convocation, we were taught the school song, which begins with this line: *"On the banks of the wide St. Johns, stands our alma mater dear . . ."*

We had crew races on the St. Johns alongside the campus. My fraternity won the first intramural rowing competition, and the crew coach even invited me to join the varsity team, but I couldn't let anything cut into my basketball time.

The river is still a favorite place for me these days. I prowl its edges and submerged treetops for the wily black bass and the tasty speckled perch. As captain of my noble vessel, the S.S. Fort Mudge, I am observer and friend to the panoply of wildlife, trees and flowers in and around the river.

Herons, 'gators, otters, anhingas, raccoons, turtles, osprey and several other critters frequent the river and its banks. Sometimes, there is even a a manatee sighting.

It is a river of dreams. A river so wonderful, and so generous with its gifts that a little jug-eared kid from Jacksonville could even build a life around it.

A gopher tortoise

Anyone Can Make
the Endangered List

The subject today is gophers. Not the groundhog kind but the tortoise type. The name of this interesting animal is often a source of confusion between Floridians and tourists.

Growing up, I believed that the wildlife of Florida was a limitless treasure. It never occurred to me that someday there wouldn't be enough for everybody. And high on my list of seemingly inexhaustible species was the lowly gopher.

I often would stop my car and pick up the slow moving animals that my folks had dubbed "gopher turtles" and sell them. It was wise to have a bucket or other easily cleaned container to keep the trapped tortoise in because they had a bad habit of, ummm, emptying their bladders very soon after capture.

Most of the buyers were older folks who remembered the hardscrabble days of the Depression when gophers were called "Hoover chickens." They became a source of much superstition and half-truth among country cousins, with claims that gopher meat had medicinal properties or would act as an aphrodisiac.

So over the years there has been unpitying and limitless trapping and killing of these docile creatures. No one growing up here ever believed there could be an end to it.

Until last year, that is, when Florida passed a law making it illegal to kill, capture, hunt or possess gopher tortoises or even pour poison or gasoline down their burrows. A couple of weeks ago, I came across a notice from the state Game and Fresh Water Fish Commission that began: "Officials have found that many Floridians still are unaware of the law."

I pride myself on being a know-it-all, but I'll 'fess up that I was one of those who never got the word. The shock of seeing something that was such a commonplace part of my youth on the endangered list sent me scurrying for a few facts about the gopher.

Thanks to Joan Diemer, the Commission's gopher tortoise biologist, those facts were easy to obtain. She explained gophers have evolved a rare characteristic among reptiles — a social structure. This lifestyle aids the tortoise in finding a mate since it rarely strays far from its home. They typically live in colonies of 10 to 20 within a 30-acre area.

Each gopher has at least one burrow, from which it emerges each day to feed on grass, leaves and berries.

When you protect the gopher, you are aiding a complex society of other little creatures, many of them endangered, which also live in the burrows, she said, such as the gopher frog and the gopher mouse, which are found nowhere else on Earth.

The gopher has a slow reproductive cycle, the biologist noted. They do not become sexually mature until about 15 years of age. During breeding season, the females lay three to seven eggs each, most of which are eaten by marauding dogs, raccoons, skunks and opossums. About 90 percent of the hatchlings do not make it past the first year.

The poor, pokey gopher is victim of growth management. Though building projects occasionally are altered to protect gopher colonies, a lot of prime tortoise habitat is being converted to human habitat.

"Wildlife officers will be investigating any reports of violations of laws protecting gopher tortoises," said Major Ron Walsingham of the commission's Panama City office. "It's important that people take the law seriously." Anyone with knowledge of anyone hunting, killing or possessing gophers should call the commission's toll-free number on the inside front cover of the telephone directory, Walsingham added.

It all gives me a guilty conscience, thinking of all the gophers I caught and sold when I was a kid.

Balladeer Sings of Bygone Days in Old-time Florida

Laziness and lack of imagination kept me from enjoying the full cup of what it was to grow up in Cracker Florida. I've seen more and heard more than the average, but you know the old problem with averages: You stick one hand in a frying pan full of hot grease and the other hand in the freezer and on the average, you're doing OK.

So there are gaping holes in my store of experiences as a Florida native. There are history lessons I slept through and times when I stayed home to watch Howdy Doody instead of getting out where I could enjoy Florida's natural bounty.

That's why I'm so grateful to my good friend, Will McLean, because I can experience through his songs and stories the pieces of Florida I missed. And he rekindles emotions that were so much a part of my childhood and made me what I am today . . . which may not be much, but I'm getting by.

It wouldn't matter to me if ole Will never had sung a lick in Carnegie Hall, which he has, or ever had a book or newspaper feature writ about him, which he has, or ever had a high-falutin' Cabinet official from Tallahassee lionize him as Florida's greatest folk balladeer, which is true.

Since I can't play a guitar or compose a melody, Will McLean does those tasks for me. I have no hope of ever acquiring the blessing/curse of the troubadour, so I depend on him.

One of the pleasures of jamborees at the Pioneer Settlement over

Barberville way is that the Friends of Florida Folk organization has agreed to provide the entertainment. For the past two years, Will has attended these jamborees and I've had the opportunity to sit a spell and get to know Will and some of his folk-singing cohorts better.

As a bonus, Will got up on stage with a couple of friends two Saturdays ago and sang one of my Florida folk favorites: "Hold Back the Waters," which chronicles the 1928 hurricane which drowned 4,000 people near Lake Okeechobee.

His songs evoke images of alligators, wild boar, Florida panther, orange blossoms, pine trees, green turtles, sandhill cranes, egrets and osprey. These stories are peopled by Seminole chiefs, military adventurers, tow-headed young'uns, kindly grandparents and assorted ne'er-do-wells.

He has written more than 3,500 songs and poems about Florida and he's still writing.

Generous to a fault, Will McLean has not profited in a big way from his talent, saying that it is a gift to the people of the state he worships.

With assistance from the Remington family in Marion County, Will has a new cassette tape of his songs titled: *"The Premiere Works of Will McLean."* Companion to this tape is a book containing some of his stories, music and lyrics. It's called *"Cross the Shadows of my Face."*

The book leads off with a wonderful reminiscence of young Will on a Huck Finn-type trek through North Florida with his grandfather. Will misses his grandpa very much, even now, and the powerful emotional tug of the closing to this story caused memories of my own granddaddy to flood back and how very precious those shared experiences were.

Will McLean and I are co-conspirators. We were fortunate to discover early in life the secrets of Florida that few visitors ever got to sample. The night-songs of the birds, catching pumpkin-seed bream on a cane pole, telling tales around the campfire about ghosts, snakes and skunk-apes, Minorcan street-singers in St. Augustine and making music on the mouth harp and gourd fiddles.

We were happy to take the part of Florida the tourists and the land-rapers didn't want, and now our Florida is the only part worth having.

Natives Feel a Longing for Pre-condo Florida

The guys in the suits call it ecotourism. It's a buzzword that makes a big deal out of a truth we Florida natives have known for years.

It is precisely the fortuitous conjunction of time, tide and temperature that fueled the untrammeled growth that has ruined parts of the state. It states the self-evident truth that folks like to reside in and visit places that are nice.

That it is fun to catch a fish, or watch an osprey swoop low over the water. Or there is solace in the roar of the surf in an early stroll along the surf line. That visitors will wait in line to watch a manatee loll around a spring just as they will queue up for Space Mountain.

I have often had contradictory thoughts about my status as an eco-resident of Florida. Sometimes I am evangelistic and beg folks to drive the Cracker Trail or take a slow boat ride up Blue Creek. Then I go into dark funks, getting secretive and curmudgeonly about our natural treasures.

It is that curious, plaintive paradox of the Florida native.

The paradox is often displayed in the music of our native Florida folk singers. I often go to festivals put on my Friends of Florida Folk and the Will McLean Foundation. Veteran Sunday Punch readers know of my respect for Will, who wrote more than 3,000 folk songs about Florida and gave them all away.

"They don't belong to me," Will would say. "They belong to the people of Florida."

Old Florida

Many of the Florida songs are dreamy. They evoke images of breezes, sand bars, the twilight chirping of chuck-will-widows. The melodies are sweet, and the words downright syrupy. These are people with serious love affairs for Florida.

Then there are those who remember what Florida used to be and are hopping mad about what has happened. Like the South Beach String Band song oft heard on the Cornbread Jamboree: *"Watch Florida grow, it's more like where did Florida go. The Florida I knew is nearly gone. Lethal yellow's killed the trees, condominiums block the breeze, and I'm having trouble understanding Brooklynese!"*

Bobby Hicks of Lake Wales, the Hank Williams Jr. of Florida folk music, is the most militant of the new breed. His most famous opus is *"The Condo Song"* in which he irreverently calls on hurricane force winds to solve the problem of large buildings blocking the ocean view.

The late Will McLean was of two minds. One evening over in Barberville, when Will paid a visit to the annual jamboree for the Pioneer Settlement, he talked of the forces that pulled at him. He understood why Bobby Hicks, whom he admired and loved greatly, is so feisty.

Will was a war hero, a World War II bomber pilot who understood some folks only respond to brute force.

But Will couldn't dwell on hateful thoughts too long. His heart, just as it was when he wrote his first song *"Away O'ee"* when he was six years old, was filled with gentler, even childlike, images.

By the campfire at the settlement or at Gore's Landing on the banks of the Oklawaha River, Will would talk of making music with the mouth harp and gourd fiddle.

Will and I shared one bond, and it was that our early lives were influenced by remarkable grandfathers. That's why I am always touched by Will's simple story of traveling North Florida with his grandpa, in that magical time when the young mind is like a sponge and soaks up the wit and wisdom of elders at a rate not duplicated at any later age.

I still am moved by a simple story Will once told. It is a metaphor for how we felt about our grandfather's generation, and for the Florida they enjoyed and we will never know. The last two sentences are:

"The man told the boy there was no tongue could tell of his love for the boy. The man was overwhelmed . . . there were no words left to say."

Another hero of Florida, the late Gamble Rogers, spoke at Will's memorial service. This is what he said about the paradox residing inside the soul of the Florida native: *"For Will McLean knew that what truly separates man from the animals is the capacity of the human heart to be divided against itself. Time and time again he bore this conflict up to us bravely and shone before us in his nakedness. Often we thought this humbled him, when it was we ourselves, who should have been humbled."*

Florida folk balladeer Will McLean and John Carter at the 1987 Pioneer Settlement Heritage Arts and Crafts Festival.

Way down upon
Suwannee River, Layoffs Happen

When I was just a little jug-eared kid growing up in Jacksonville, my elementary schoolteachers were big on field trips.

We went to the bakery, following a loaf of bread down the assembly line. The Jacksonville Zoo, which I remember today mainly for the horde of hideously screeching peacocks who walked the grounds, was on the itinerary.

We toured the water plant, making sure we were there at lunchtime to get an ear-splitting blast from the noon whistle, which Jaxons had dubbed "Big Jim."

But our little pea-brains were most impressed by an out-of-town trip. One day we went to the Stephen Foster Memorial at White Springs.

This is a tribute to a man who never went to Florida and died penniless in a freezing hovel in New York. He originally wrote a song titled *"Way Down Upon the Pee Dee River,"* but then his finger wandered down the map until he found a Florida stream called the Suwannee.

Because of Stephen Foster, the Suwannee River became one of the best known rivers in the world, especially in the minstrel, vaudeville and choral music shows that were the rage in those days.

That field trip made an indelible imprint on me. It made me hungry to know more about Florida history and created a soft spot in my heart for the charming little burg of White Springs.

Well, there is no joy in White Springs these days, because that moss-draped little hamlet of my boyhood reveries has lost one of its biggest industries.

We're only talking about 10 employees and a $550,000 budget here, but in its own way, the loss is as big as the neutron bomb that hit Volusia County the year Martin Marietta pulled up stakes.

Secretary of State Sandra Mortham said last week that by the end of the year, she will shut down the Bureau of Florida Folklife in White Springs, lay off three employees and move the remaining seven jobs to Tallahassee.

I like the Bureau of Florida Folklife.

One of the employees there, Barbara Beauchamp, was such a sweetheart the time I wandered in looking for background stuff on Zora Neale Hurston.

It was Barbara who handed me a set of cassette tapes with recordings of Zora singing turpentine camp songs (some of them X-rated) collected during a Depression-era anthropological foray.

So, I called Margaret Longhill, founder of the Will McLean Foundation, and a person whose love for Florida is boundless.

Bless her heart, Margaret provided soothing and wise words that calmed me down. These changes, she explained, have been discussed quite a bit by our historians, folk singers and artists.

Now, the community has decided to give this reorganization a chance, Margaret said. She told me that conversations with Secretary Mortham have been cordial and she appears willing to listen to the Florida native view-point in cultural affairs.

Well, I was mellowing out, pondering the wise words, when I got a fax from Secretary Mortham her own se'f, assuring me that the White Springs happenings were part of an effort to save the folklife program, not to destroy it.

"In the budget reduction talks of the past two years the Bureau of Folklife, along with the historic preservation boards, has become a common target for some legislator," Secretary Mortham wrote. *"The reorganization of the folklife program, saving approximately $75,000 a year, may in fact save the program from complete elimination."*

I'm still going to miss those nifty little trips to White Springs.

Etymology of Our County: Does Anyone Have a Clue?

Volusia, my Volusia. Most Florida counties are named for presidents, soldiers, politicians, tycoons, Indians and bodies of water. We manage to get the only county name which has no known origin.

Volusia — a name enshrouded in mystery. It looks funny. Sounds funny. Nobody knows how we got it. This is a terrible situation ripe for the ravings of conspiracy theorists.

There are places in Mesopotamia that predate everything but the first few verses of Genesis, and their citizens know how and why the places were named. The name "Volusia" first popped up as a reference to our beloved area in the 1820s or 1830s, which is before we were born but hardly the Dark Ages.

A few brave souls have attempted to write the history of Volusia County despite the inevitable slings and arrows of carping criticism from old-timers. They threw up their hands when it came time to write the obligatory paragraph on the origin of the county name.

Some of the theories were pretty lame. Could have come from a Belgian trader named Veluche, they noted. Maybe an old Indian word. The middle name of a Roman nobleman?

I think we can do better than that. If we're doomed never to know how our county got its name, then we at least ought to have more interesting folk tales and lies. This could be the beginning of an important historical project, and I've always had a secret desire to be a historian. To get the ball rolling, I'll share with you a couple of my pet theories about Volusia etymology.

Based on reports from the noted scout and river scumrat Churchy LaFemme, there once was a tribe of invisible Indians, known as the Volusia, who settled near the present day site of the Seabreeze traffic circle. To this day, not a single trace of these invisible Indians has ever been found. *"Sheer proof that they existed,"* Churchy crayoned into his diary.

Another theory is promulgated by the Russians, who claim they discovered Volusia County during a period of great exploration by Soviet adventurers. Count Yegevny Aisulov declared the lands east of the St. Johns River to be the property of the czar, but the bourgeois, no account Count quickly left the area when confronted by moonshiners and a sheriff who felt one czar in the county was enough. He later was credited by the Soviet government with opening trade routes to Kazakhstan, discovering salt in Siberia and the invention of Saran Wrap. Aisulov, of course, spelled backwards is "Natures," er, I mean, "Volusia."

According to the best seller *"Pick Up Trucks of the Gods,"* by Erich von Danskins, our county first was inhabited by visitors from the planet Volus, a few light years southwest of Betelguese, and the Volusians brought us many features of their world, such as timesharing, beach ramp tolls and senior citizen discounts. They returned to their home galaxy after a brief layover in Atlanta.

I invite readers to come up with explanations of how our county picked up the Volusia moniker. I'll print some of them and pass the others around the office. It's about time we had a county name with a rich history, one that instills pride and is worth telling in a cement floor bar.

Up to now the only nice thing about Volusia is that it's a vast improvement over one of the previous names for this area — Mosquito County. And we know where that one came from.

Missing the Man
Who Knew Everything

One of the nicest things my friend Carl Laundrie ever did was to introduce me to Otis Hunter.

It was back in 1986 when I became curious about that charming narrow red-brick road that runs through the pine scrub from Espa'ola to Hastings.

I asked Carl, the top gun in our Flagler Bureau, to recommend someone as a source for data on the brick road and about the glory days of Espa'ola and he nominated Otis Hunter, by actual vote a former commissioner of Flagler County and by general acclamation the "Mayor of Espa'ola."

Anytime folks needed some information about Flagler geography or genealogy, sooner or later they were told to, "Go ask Otis," or in country parlance, "Drop by and see if Otis is to the house."

That's what Carl and I did one Christmas Eve. We dropped by to see Otis and he was there, walking around doing some minor chores while barefoot, in bluejeans and a pajama top. He put a pot on on the stove, the old-fashioned percolator kind, and made some strong coffee.

I was impressed with his wonderful sense of time and place. Otis lived less than a mile from the place where he was born in 1920 and not much farther from where his daddy was born in 1888.

With steaming cups of java in hand, we wandered out into the yard, where Otis had a small museum going. Actually, his wife had laid down the law and told him to get all that clutter out of the house.

70

The little shed was a jumble of old bottles, antique farm equipment, quaint signs, arrowheads, pottery, gewgaws and gimcracks.

The talk soon shifted to the reason I had come to learn more about Espa'ola and the red brick road. Once upon a time, before there was a U.S. 1, the main north-south route through this area was the Dixie Highway. The nine-foot-wide road was built in 1916 and for a decade was touted as part of the tourist route "from Maine to Miami."

Otis and other Espa'ola boys used to play tricks on the "tin-can tourists" who drove by pulling those shiny silver trailers that were popular back then. Espa'ola was something to see in those days, with hotels, a barber shop and all sorts of other thriving businesses.

That road, by the way, is still passable. It is possible to go all the way to Hastings on it, as long as you watch for the damage made by logging trucks and the places where thieves have stolen bricks.

Bunnell captured the county seat and the route for U.S. 1 and the boom went bust in Espa'ola.

Otis and his family never shed any tears about that.

"There's plenty of people out here right now, as far as I'm concerned," he once told me.

I asked why he tired of politics after decades of service.

"I just got tired of it," he said with a shrug, "Palm Coast got too big for me."

Fast forward as those of us who love Florida, who don't mind all that much if our home town doesn't grow and who give a damn about that charming red brick road in the piney woods, grieve over the loss of Otis Hunter.

He died Tuesday at Memorial Hospital-Flagler. In his obituary, many of his achievements were listed and some nice Flagler folks responded to our request to tell us what they thought of Otis.

But just before I sat down to write this column, we got a wonderful phone call from the Otis Hunter family. They told us the article we ran on his life and death was perfect, and the family appreciated the work we did on it.

I'm not surprised at that. The example has been set, and they are now carrying the torch of kindness, intelligence and love of country that Otis Hunter bore with such grace.

Moved to Tears by a War Nobody Won

Back when I was a little jug-eared kid growing up in Jacksonville, I padded into our Florida room on West Tenth Street and found my grandmother sitting in an easy chair crying.

Her crochet needles were resting on her lap, and she was dabbing at a tear on her cheek. I was only nine or ten years old and I was very worried about her and asked what was wrong.

"Oh, it's OK, son," she reassured me. "I was just sitting here thinking about how the South lost the Civil War."

Another anecdote: My grandfather once asked me to walk to our bank to make a deposit. When I got there, the door was locked and a sign proclaimed: "Closed for Robert E. Lee's Birthday."

Jacksonville also boasted a Robert E. Lee High School and I attended Edmund Kirby-Smith Junior High, where I learned most of the impudence and bad jokes I still exhibit today. There was a Confederate Park and many monuments to the men in gray.

There was a plaque downtown with the shameful news that the city once was occupied by the Union, but a joyous footnote that the Yankees had been repulsed at Olustee, leaving Tallahassee as the only Confederate capital which never felt the oppressor's boot.

The school curriculum was no less one-sided, giving an account of the mid-1850s heavy on John C. Calhoun and light on Henry Clay, and leaving a feeling about the outcome of the war similar to that tearful lament of my grandmother.

There were no debates about display of the Confederate Battle Flag those days. Full-throated Rebel Yells were encouraged and everyone stood when "Dixie" was played, just as if it were the National Anthem.

I had no frame of reference to handle this overwhelming flood of gray. I was a Rebel without a clue.

It was not until I was in college and also in a military history class in Officer Candidate School that I received a less-biased interpretation of that unhappy war. Though I'm far from a scholar of that conflict, it still holds a strange fascination fro me.

I was visiting my son, daughter-in-law and grandson in Sheperdstown, West Virginia, last month. That historic little village is across the Potomac from the Maryland town of Sharpsburg, which was the focus for the Battle of Antietam.

I had read about Antietam many times and even had played a computer simulation of it a few years ago. Having toured some other Civil War battlefields in past years, I was very surprised at what I saw.

When you see how small the area is and visualize about 85,000 federals and 35,000 rebs crammed into it, then it becomes clear how September 17, 1862 became the bloodiest day in American military history. There were more than 20,000 casualties in a battle now known for the costly miscalculations by both sides.

The saddest thing about Antietam is that both sides lost and yet both sides pretended they won. The rebels were heartened by their stalemate with a numerically superior force and found the vigor to fight three more years.

Union soldiers rejoiced in saving Washington, and President Lincoln used it as a pretext for issuing the Emancipation Proclamation.

We walked through the battleground museum, looking at the artifacts and the storyboards of men who fought there and even brave women, such as Clara Barton, who served. While driving through the park, we turned on an impulse to a little circle in the West Woods, where at dawn troops serving for two of the most aggressive commanders in the war clashed.

"Fighting Joe" Hooker sent his units against defenders' commander "Stonewall" Jackson. Both deserved their nicknames. Jackson had rushed to the far side of the field after taking Harper's Ferry.

Old Florida

A fully little twinge of wonderment and sadness came over me as I stood by a white obelisk marking a spot where 1,000 men fell in only 30 minutes of furious combat.

The tour had been a dry academic exercise until that point, but I was moved nearly to tears at that moment, not because the South had lost the Civil War, but that those poor scared boys from both sides had died in a battle which nobody lost and nobody won.

The Jug-eared Kid

I came along too late to derive maximum benefits from non-stick frying pans, clear plastic wrap, creamy peanut butter, microwave French fries, computer games and electronic fish locators.

— JC

Trip to Hometown Brings back Family Memories

Took another spin up to my hometown of Jacksonville last week. The world's largest village is still under repair and looks nothing like the friendly little town I once knew.

The sprawl to the south is pretty severe. I'm still not used to the sound of someone talking about Mandarin, Orange Park, Green Cove Springs and Doctor's Inlet as if they are almost downtown.

When I was just a little jug-eared kid, the family would take leisurely Sunday drives to Mandarin. We would slow down on streets framed with moss-draped oaks, stopping at roadside stands where residents were selling home-grown citrus.

My favorite was a tart treat called a satsuma. It peeled like a tangerine, but was a lot larger, so you got more for your money.

Weather and real estate developers eventually erased Mandarin's tiny citrus industry and I doubt a satsuma can be found within a hundred miles of there today.

You can, however, buy a Big Mac, a Whopper or a pizza with cheese in the crust.

Black Creek, near Doctor's Inlet, was where I caught my first fish, a little stumpknocker who gulped the worm I dropped through a hole in the hyacinths.

I don't remember it because I was so little, but my grandparents delighted in telling and retelling how I yelled and laughed as the poor little "brim" not much larger than my hand flopped around in the grass.

They then told how they fried the little fish up to a golden brown, set it apart from the rest of the day's catch, and let me pour ketchup over it and feast on my first piscatorial prize.

In the Carter clan, the first fish had a status reserved for first communions, bar mitzvahs and baptisms in other families.

A typical fishing excursion with H.D. was a mixture of joy and dread. It was always fun to be around him and we were the best buddies.

But the downside was that I was a slugabed and H.D. liked to get going around 4 a.m. or so.

By the time I slipped on jeans and a T-shirt, H.D. was sitting in the kitchen, fully dressed and working on a cup of coffee.

As he finished the coffee, I was sent to the shed to get our three horsepower Wizard outboard motor and its gas can, some cane poles, a tackle box and assorted other gear into our pickup truck.

H.D. then came out clutching a bag packed with sardines, deviled ham, Beanie Weenie, thermos of coffee, jug of water, saltine crackers and Vi-enner sausages.

We drove empty streets south to the Doctor's Inlet bridge, and on to a small, ramshackle fish camp on Black Creek.

We rented a boat, put the Wizard on it and fired it up. We never burned much gas, because H.D. never saw a clump of grass or raft of hyacinth that he didn't like.

He always wanted to dab an earthworm, cricket or minnow in the next hole in the weeds. Anyone fishing with H.D. spent most of his day guiding the boat and putting it into position while H.D. fished.

It was a routine that many members of our family went through, but we all loved it, and we still laugh about it today.

Anytime I hear a politician or preacher rattle on about "family values" I wonder if they really know what they're talking about.

H.D. Carter was the best damned value a family ever had.

Two Proud Little Jug-eared Kids

Every society has its rites of passage. You don't have to be a Margaret Mead to know that most tribes of this Earth have important ceremonies or customs which identify which children are ready to assume the responsibilities and rights of adulthood.

Redneck families such as mine have such rites, it's just harder to isolate them and index them from the bewildering welter of superstitions (some would say ignorances), nostrums and potions which combine to produce the great wad which calls itself the great American lower to middle class.

My family also has set great store by fishing as a healthy and productive activity for our young'uns. Some of you may spend many hours relating where you were when Pearl Harbor was attacked, or what you were doing when JFK was shot, but the Carter clan considers those events secondary to memories of the day each of us caught his or her first fish.

My folks have been far from perfect. Many lived quiet and respectable lives of honesty and industriousness, but truth to tell there were a rotten few that were in that southern fried category whispered about conspiratorially as "white trash."

It never occurred to the patriarchs and matriarchs of my family that the bad apples among us — the jailbirds, hookers, petty con men, bar room scufflers and prescription drug junkies — once had caught a first fish too. It was family gospel that fishing was good for you and made one respectable, upright and a good American, and that was that!

When a child is told something many times by adults, pretty soon a lively imagination takes over and the poor tyke begins believing he actually recalls it. My mind is full of such incidents about which I am confused, because of constant repetition of stories about my toddlerhood.

Anyway, I either remember or was told that a little red-eared sunfish, a stumpknocker in good ole boy talk, took the hook and pulled the small cork under. I pulled the flopping fish out of the water and let out a great whoop which caused all grandparents, uncles, aunts and cousins to come running.

Pictures were taken of this unfortunate fish, and my grandmother was careful to keep track of the little stumpknocker as she fried the day's catch for dinner that night. I was one proud little jug-eared kid as I ate the crunchy little sunfish while the family beamed with pride.

I never figured out what all the fuss was about until one day about 20 years later when I took my son, David, then barely big enough to wind a rod and reel, fishing off of a dock on the St. Johns River just south of Palatka. I taught him how to place a minnow on the hook and then I walked back to the trailer.

About 15 minutes later I heard David cut loose with a loud whoop and by the time I ran to the dock he had a large speckled perch, dern near a two pound slab, almost out of the water. I don't know if David remembers this or not, but we took great care to make sure we could identify his first fish as we fried up a few that night.

Nestled up next to the cole slaw, hush puppies and grits laced with drippings from the grease we had fried the fish in was a big hunk of the speckled perch. He was one proud little jug-eared kid as he chomped down on that fish. By flickering lantern light, Dad and the rest of the clan beamed with pride. Then I understood.

Growing up Lefthanded

This is a very gauche and sinister story. Those of you familiar with the slanderous French and Latin roots of those adjectives will know that the theme of this week's offering is growing up lefthanded in a righthanded world.

I shouldn't have to recount to you all the discrimination we southpaws have to endure in this world. We get the side of the bowling alley still slick with oil, the blank corners of the playing cards and only Jimi Hendrix and Paul McCartney knew how we manage to play a guitar.

Our left to right writing tradition is an example of the ingrained raw deal suffered by portsiders. The reason we learned to curl our hand and wrist around and over the line is to avoid smearing the ink as the left hand travels across the page.

Righthanders never had to put up with those telltale ink smudges on the side of the hand.

My first grade teacher at Beulah Beal Elementary School on Ninth Street in Jacksonville believed that lefthanders needed special attention in penmanship. On the first day of school, Mrs. Powell announced to an awestruck and terrified group of kids that she wanted the lefthanders to be culled from the group — separating the sheep from the goats and the wheat from the chaff.

Even at six years old I was already aware that I was on the left hand of God, but I'll be darned if I was going to end up on the left hand of Mrs. Powell. I kept my hand down, looking around the room to see if there were any other lefthanders in the class.

There was. One. A shy little pink-frocked girl with a missing front tooth raised her hand. Her name was Rose.

Squrrawk . . . Mrs. Powell dragged a desk across the wooden floor apart from the rest and motioned for Rose to move to the new desk. The plot now became clear. If I were uncovered as a sinistral gaucherie, two bad things would happen.

"Self," I said to my fearful first day of school self, "Self, if you raise your hand you will be separated from the safety of the herd and, now hear this, YOU WILL HAVE TO SIT NEXT TO A GIRL FOR THE WHOLE SCHOOL YEAR. A GIRL! YOU HEAR THAT! A GIRL!!"

I dummied up. For weeks, I carefully maintained my little subterfuge. Anytime Mrs. Powell was looking, I colored in coloring books or penciled on copy paper with my right hand. If her head was turned or attention focused elsewhere, I switched the pencil or crayon to my left hand and tried to get as much work done as I could before being forced back into dextral mode.

Well, heck, I'm not all that bright now and I was a really naive six year old. One day I was moving like sixty, lefthanded, across a page writing capitals and lowers from the alphabet across sheets of that paper with the extra wide lines on it, when suddenly I sensed trouble.

Mrs. Powell stood slightly behind my desk, lips pursed, foot tapping. She didn't say a word. She didn't have to. I knew I was doomed.

Squrrawk . . . Another desk was pulled across splintery boards, and the sound tore at my heart like the red eyed hounds of hell. Mrs. Powell's firm right hand grabbed my left shoulder, and I don't even remember if my feet touched the floor as I was deposited next to the previously solitary and now second hand Rose.

She wasn't exactly thrilled at the prospect of sitting next to me for the rest of the term. I wonder whatever happened to her and if her writing ever improved, and does she always color within the lines?

As for me, I have terrible penmanship and never could stay between the lines. My book of life is a dot to dot book, as yet unconnected. But I have an alibi. First Grade trauma, pure and simple.

Cotton Pickin', Melon Bustin' Days of June

When I was but a jug-eared kid trapped in a school-room while outside the sun was shining and the birds were tweeting, I thought it ironic that the teacher had us read these lines from Lowell's *"Vision of Sir Launfal"*:

"And what is so rare as a day in June? Then, if ever, come perfect days."

Yeah, and the best part was that school was out. Who can forget the sounds that erupted from the classrooms and halls when that last bell rang and hundreds of hellions were loosed on an unsuspecting community for a whole summer?

YAAAYYY! The roar bounced up and down stairwells and then rushed out the door. People who lived in the homes near the school knew what that sound meant. It was the signal for another three months of having kids take shortcuts through your yard, hearing baseballs bounce off your roof and having little urchins steal cool drinks of water from your garden hose.

Those perfect June days to me consisted of visiting the Springfield Library and trying to read every book in the place if I could, and sitting through some really nifty Tuesday night travelog programs. Sometimes the librarian, who actually loved little jug-eared kids and never shushed them or made us sit real still, would serve cookies and Kool-Aid.

June was the month for sleeping late and staying up late and not having any adults make a big fuss out of it. Instead of homework, there was piddling around the back shed, getting fishing tackle in shape and tinkering with that old Wizard outboard motor.

Most summers, my grandfather would ship me off to visit with our Georgia kin, in line with his theory that farm work would "make a man" out of me and also encourage me to study harder in school so I wouldn't have to work on a farm when I was grown.

But June days in Georgia could be fun. There was bustin' water-melons, of course, and we would go through the fields thumping the melons and eating only the seedless "hearts" out of the ones that passed our thumping test. Sometimes we would get into my Uncle David's favorite field of "yaller meat" watermelons that had a pale, near orange middle as sweet as spun sugar.

Uncle David never got mad. He just scratched his head and remembered when he was a jug-eared kit and enjoyed bustin' a watermelon or two his own se'f.

The closest I came to learning the lesson my grandfather intended was when I would be conscripted for labor in the cotton patch. Wearing a flannel shirt, big overalls and a big straw hat in the midday June heat, I dragged this huge, flowing croaker sack behind me down the rows of cotton.

My first day, I started out with a bang. I was picking cotton faster than anybody in the field. That's when I learned you are supposed to pace yourself and that the tortoise did indeed win the race with the hare. Less than an hour after I got there, my energy was gone, and my rear end was dragging as much as that oversized croaker sack.

I made several trips to the ice water jug, but nothing helped.

It's become one of the knee-slapping family stories to tell people what my face looked like when the boss weighed in my cotton that day as he put a quarter and a dime — 35 lousy cents — in my tired, grubby palm.

I wanted to tell ole Sir Launfal that it's easy to talk about perfect June days when you are hot on the trail of the Holy Grail. It's flat-out somethin' else when it's cotton-pickin' time in South Georgia.

Train Man Memories
Conjure Sadness, Joy

One of the favorite characters of my childhood was the Train Man.

If we had more time, I would assure you of my concern for the homeless and the deinstitutionalized mentally ill because there is as much sadness as joy in the story of Jacksonville's Train Man.

When I was a kid, there was only the joy. It's only now that I recognize Train Man as one of those for whom life was a cup and saucer short of a full place setting.

Everyone in Jacksonville knew Train Man, although there aren't many who ever knew his name. My late grandfather knew Train Man quite well, and by name, but the attempts I've made this week to recall the name have been hopeless.

The Train Man had worked for the railroad. When the company told him he was retired and put him on a pension, something in the Train Man's head snapped. Though he was barred from working on real trains, he strung several red wagons, the American Flyer types popular in the 1940s and '50s, and pulled them down the streets of Jacksonville.

He wore gray twill bib overalls and a matching engineer's cap. Sometimes his wife would be a passenger, sitting in one of the red wagons with her massive thighs bulging over the edges.

He would stop every now and then and play records on an old windup Victrola he transported in the caboose wagon. The Victrola used steel needles, and if the record sounded a bit scratchy (it always

85

did), Train Man would remove the tone arm and replace the needle.

"There. Thass better," he would announce with a big smile. I never could notice any improvement. Then I found out why. Train Man owned only two steel needles, and he kept switching them.

Train Man often came by the front of my granddaddy's furniture store on Old Kings Road. He was a strong and indefatigable hiker, pulling his red wagon train from as far away as Baldwin.

Granddad always kept several Coca-Colas in the old six-ounce bottles in the refrigerator in the back of the store. Like many Jaxons, he called them "Co-Colas."

It was his custom to give the Train Man, and Mrs. Train Man, too, a Co-Cola anytime they were in the Old Kings Road area. Train Man would gratefully accept, empty the bottle in an unbroken series of gulps just like you see in the commercials, then play a record in our honor.

One day when Train Man came by, my granddaddy was busy and didn't see him. But I did. I grabbed two Co-Colas from the refrigerator and ran to the front door. He was halfway down the block when I yelled: "Hey! Train Man!"

He turned and acknowledge my call: "I'll be right there direckly, Mistuh Jawn."

I discovered a terrible truth about Train Man. They were only little red wagons to me, but to him they were real railroad cars, and they were ON TRACKS! He couldn't turn around and come back to the front door of the store. He had to back up on his imaginary tracks.

He wouldn't let me bring the drinks to where he was. He would try to back up the string of wagons until they would buckle and start accordioning to one side. He would straighten them out and try to back them up again.

Each attempt brought him only an inch or two closer to the store. I tried to tell him to stop, but he wouldn't. When at last he arrived at the storefront, he took the Co-Colas, gave one to his wife and he quickly downed the other.

I felt rotten that I had caused such trouble and kept apologizing, but he just smiled, thanked me as he doffed his engineer's cap and played me a tune on that old Victrola.

A Marvel Known as Television

In August 1949, I was one of the most popular little jug-eared kids in the Springfield neighborhood of Jacksonville. Kids, and their moms and dads too, would knock at the door and shyly ask if they could see the treasure sitting in the den of my West 10th Street abode.

Taking advantage of his status as a furniture dealer, my grandfather had purchased at wholesale a 19-inch RCA television set. It is only for the youngest of readers that I point out it was a black and white model, and not color.

News that there was a television set on the block gave us a sort of instant celebrity status. Folks would stop me on the street and ask me about it and I would shrug and say what it did mostly was sit there.

That's because we got our set two months before there was a television station broadcasting a signal in Jacksonville. If we turned it on at all, it was to stare at snow. As the day for the first broadcast neared, we got to watch what we thought was a pretty neat test pattern.

I remember the first day we saw the test pattern we called Miss Edna Conatser, the school teacher who rented an upstairs apartment from us, to come see. At night, we would sometimes flip on the set to see if the test pattern was on while we were listening to our favorite radio serials, like Gangbusters, Mr. Keen, Tracer of Lost Persons, Inner Sanctum and The Shadow.

In our excitement, we didn't realize the seeds of destruction of the classic radio serial already had taken firm root in the blank cathode ray tube that would dominate our thoughts and lives even before there was anything to watch.

Weeks passed, which seemed like years to a nine-year-old kid. Then it happened. We turned on the set, fiddled with the knobs and got a picture. I forgot about basketball at Springfield Park or playing sandlot football in the empty lot next to the library.

I was a regular at the Tuesday night travel movies at the library. But I was so mesmerized by the tube, I missed a couple of travelogue adventures.

The station was on only a few hours a day at first, but I watched every blurry film. I don't remember any of them except that there were several episodes of "Captain Winslow of the Marines" and "Nyoka the Jungle Girl."

My grandfather remained aloof. He was waiting for the day when his favorite radio show came to live on the screen. For years, ole H.D. Carter had been a loyal follower of Brace Beemer's radio Lone Ranger. "From out of the pages of yesteryear, come the thundering hoofbeats of the great horse Silver . . ."

Now he became the willing disciple of the Lone Ranger series featuring Clayton Moore as the masked rider of the plains and Jay Silverheels as his faithful sidekick, Tonto.

When the station added video versions of such radio staples as "One Man's Family" and "Our Miss Brooks," my grandmother also was hooked.

Fortunately, all of us eventually learned to "Just Say No" to the tube and get out and live life and read books, magazines and newspapers. But for one brief heady moment, the Carter clan of Jacksonville was plugged in to an all consuming trend.

Marshall McLuhan was right. The medium was so much more important than the message that folks for blocks around would travel to see a piece of furniture in a Florida cracker home and marvel at it.

I still marvel, but for a much different reason.

Kids Today Don't Know
What They're Missing

I pity the youngsters of today. Saturday mornings are pretty tame, thanks to the very unimaginative, overcommercialized and silly collection of cartoon offerings by the major networks.

Our small fry spend a lot of weekend hours "just hanging out" or trying to figure out what they want to do. When I was a youngster in Jacksonville, one of the holy terrors of 10th Street, there was no doubt about the agenda.

I was one of the rowdy regulars of the Capitol Theater near 8th and Main. For nine cents admission, plus a few nickels for popcorn, cola, grape or orange drinks, licorice whips, Black Crows, Ju-jubes, Milk Duds, Sugar Daddys, Goobers, Raisinettes or Kandy Korn, you could zap dern near the entire morning and afternoon.

It was cheap entertainment. I often left home with no money in my jeans, stopping at homes between 10th and 8th Streets, knocking on the doors and asking if anyone had any spare pop bottles or coat hangers. Next to the theater was a dry cleaning shop with a kindly lady who would give me a penny for every two hangers I could provide. On the other side was a small grocery store run by an immigrant family named Bateh. In broken English, Mr. Bateh would ask if I had purchased the bottles from his store, and I would lie and say that I had.

He would frown and give me two cents for each small bottle and a nickel for each quarter container. I would never look back as I left.

Old Bateh always made you feel that redeeming soft drink bottles

89

was some kind of crime.

I ran for the box office, plunked the coins down and elbowed my way to the glass case of the concession stand. I'd then go into the gloomy darkness and find a seat, my little feet slipping on the floor icky with popcorn oil and spilled burgundy grape drinks.

The noise of hundreds of kids screaming, teasing and fighting each other echoed through the theater. Then a shaft of light from the projection booth, a blast of sound and the curtain began to open. From the throats of more six to 12 year olds than you would ever want to meet in your whole life came a resounding: YAAAYYYyyyyy!

A typical Saturday playbill at the Capitol began with Chapter 7 of Nyoka the Jungle Girl, The Mark of Zorro or Captain Winslow of the Marines. Then came two, sometimes three, cartoons. Bugs Bunny, Mickey Mouse, Goofy, Elmer Fudd, Woody Woodpecker, Droopy, Tom & Jerry and some of the first Roadrunner cartoons filled the screen. They were genuinely funny, and who cares if they contained graphic depictions of violence?

The movies were usually westerns — double features or triple headers. Once in a while there would be a detective story or a pirate adventure, but westerns were our passion.

Roy Rogers, Gene Autry, Rex Allen, the Durango Kid, Randolph Scott, Gabby Hayes, Smiley Burnette and Andy Devine wore the white hats. We booed and hissed amazingly inept villains such as Barton MacLane and I. Stanford Jolley who couldn't shoot straight and who rode slow horses.

Not all of the entertainment was on the screen. We heaped catcalls and other verbal abuse on Jack Dew, the white haired emcee who walked on stage and announced a drawing of ticket stubs for prizes, such as a new bicycle. I never won a bicycle and neither did any of my friends and classmates. We always assumed that it was fixed and that the two-wheeler went to Jack Dew's niece.

One Saturday afternoon, when I was about 10 or 11 years old, I wrote my name into Capitol Theater history. I flattened out my popcorn box and sailed it through the air, Frisbee style. The box made a graceful arc through the light from the projector and then stuck.

Thunk!, like a dart into the screen.

I acknowledged the wild cheers of my peers as a stern-visaged usher yanked me from my seat and escorted me out. For months afterward, I was a pint-sized celebrity at Beulah Beal Elementary. Being thrown out of the Capitol was a great honor and I'm probably the only little jug-eared kid who ever succeeded in sticking a popcorn box into the screen.

Nothing I've done since has given me as much satisfaction.

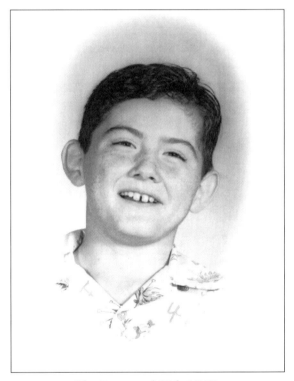

The Jug-eared Kid, 1948.

Pop's a Lost Paradise

Pop's Drugstore at 10th and Pearl was the unofficial headquarters of my Jacksonville boyhood. There really was a proprietor named Pop, a short, wizened guy who always wore an apron and had a gift for making the best hot fudge sundaes, strawberry shortcakes, banana splits, chocolate milkshakes and phosphates this side of calorie heaven.

The store had one of those neat, old-fashioned soda fountains, with stools you could spin around on until someone screamed at you to stop and the heavy, cold marble just made for propping elbows on. There were little marble tables scattered around with small chairs which had wire backs which were shaped like hearts, sort of.

We used to hang out there even when we had no money, and if challenged to order something by the ever watchful management, we'd sarcastically ask for a "pine float," which was a toothpick floating in a glass of water.

Though it was heaven for us, we neighborhood urchins made life hell for the long-suffering Pop. The poor man spent most of his life shooing us away from the comic book racks, which we treated as sort of a lending library, and the rest of the time stopping us from cheating the pinball machine.

None of us, to my recollection, ever shoplifted any comic books or magazines from the big book rack which took up almost an entire wall. Heck, we didn't have to. We'd just squat down on the floor with a couple of comic books, read them and then put them back on the rack for other kids to come in and read later.

That's where I came to know and love such comic creations as Sad Sack, Krazy Kat, Batman, Superman, Captain Marvel and Tales From The Crypt.

People sometimes ask me if I ever had a comic book collection when I was a kid. Not really. I read most of 'em for free over at Pop's.

Fame comes in strange packages sometimes. I had major league bragging rights among the grimy, shirtless and barefooted ragamuffins of Springfield because I once put the pinball machine up on the tops of my feet and racked up 24 free games before Pop discovered what was literally afoot, and rushed over the chastise me.

Sometimes we would travel in a wolfpack, storm the store and keep Pop occupied while one of us would put in a nickel, run up a couple of free games on the machine and we would play all afternoon, squabbling with each other who would get to play the next ball.

A pretty good day's entertainment for only a nickel.

If sociologists and culture vultures someday ever do any research on the disappearance of the neighborhood drugstore and how it got replaced by the big chains which actually are department stores in disguise, I'll be glad to testify how it all happened.

The Springfield irregulars — dirty-faced little jug-eared kids like yours truly, put Pop out of business and killed the neighborhood store. It's a great loss but we have no one to blame but ourselves.

Stinky Girls Just Weren't Fair to Jug-eared Kid

Back in 1947, I was a second-grader at Brentwood Elementary School in Jacksonville. We lived on West 23rd Street and it was a great neighborhood. I had it all: walking distance to the Brentwood Theater, a drugstore with a full soda fountain one block to the south and a fire station with a regulation-sized pool table a block north. An easy bike ride west was Brentwood Park, where we played pick-up football and basketball games.

The firemen sort of "adopted" the neighborhood urchins, and would let us upstairs to shoot pool if we promised not to rip the baize fabric, and then we'd slide down the fire pole to the ground floor.

If there were no fire calls and all the brass had been polished, the firefighters would dig out the broomsticks and corkballs, and we would have stickball tournaments right in the middle of Perry Street, stopping occasionally to allow a passing car to go by.

The fireman taught me how to make a corkball, by wrapping tape around a fishing cork with a penny on one end to make it curve, dip and dart, depending on how you released it. I had a real aptitude for the knuckleball delivery and I soon became the best pitcher on the street.

The teams were made up of one fireman and one urchin for a typical two-man game, with storm sewers and trees marking the limits for singles, doubles, triples and homers.

The urchins improved until one day we were forming teams to play

94

against the adults.

A Jacksonville policeman lived across the street from us, and I became buddies with his two sons, Terry and Ronnie.

Ronnie was my age, and we became a team. Actually, we could beat the firemen at corkball and he had neat pets like baby squirrels, turtles and snakes and things. Maybe it was at that age he formed the mindset that led him to grow up to be a leading state expert on fire safety, which some folks tell me he did.

There was no thought of political correctness in 1947 and it would have been hooted down with belly laughs if it had surfaced. Many days after school or on weekends, Ronnie and I would haul our cap pistols and holsters from the toy box and spend a few hours "playing guns."

Sometimes, we would limit the game to 23rd Street. Other times, the territory would be wider and extend past the drugstore and fire station. As we played, other neighborhood urchins would ask to join the game, and we usually said OK.

Unless, of course, the kid pleading for a spot in the game was a stinky old girl!

This, also, is a massive dose of political incorrectness, but Ronnie and I learned early on that girls were poison in a classic game of "guns." They were clumsy players and never really knew any good ambush points, but it didn't matter, because they had one nagging attribute...

They wouldn't die.

That's right. There was nothing a little boy loved better than a death scene of Shakespearean proportions. We would clutch at our little pigeon chests, squeeze off a random shot into the air, give out a long, dramatic moan, spin around twice and then fall in a heap on the ground, twitching three or four times for added dramatic effect.

I never saw a girl do that. In fact, you could jump from a hiding place, and put your cap gun against a girls' head and pull the trigger. After the cap popped, the girl would turn around with a smug smile, and say: "Hah! You missed!"

Then she would fire her cap gun, and argue with you if there was any complaint about "not playing fair."

I've recounted this history many times to a female friend, who always defends the fair sex from this dastardly charge. "You're just jealous because girls can always get the drop on boys in a game of guns," she says, in a voice that reminds me very much of the haughty tone I once heard in "Hah! Missed!"

Things are more like they are now than they've ever been before. I once thought Dwight Eisenhower was silly for saying that but I've since some to know very well what it means.

Never play guns with girls.

Second grade, 1948

Carters and Clodhoppers: What a pair

Big feet run in my family. You might say this week's episode of Sunday Punch is titled: "The Curse of the Carter Clodhoppers."

What makes it even worse is that it's not just male members of the clan who suffer from humongous hoof syndrome, but the demure wimmenfolk as well. Only my dainty daughter, Karen, has escaped...she being the only Carter who wears shoes that are smaller than a shoebox.

Speaking of shoeboxes, I once was the object of well-meaning but cruel jests from my grandfather. He was a size nine. I was born size 12 and then grew into my feet, sort of like a beagle puppy or a Clydesdale horse, I reckon.

Anyhow, my grandpa would suggest that I "throw away the shoes and wear the boxes."

Shoes played a big part in my growing-up years, which might explain why I am so careless about them now. I always wanted casual footwear, like penny loafers, mocassins with tassels and tennis shoes (not the new designer type tennis shoes, but the old-fashioned black hightop models.)

My grandfather always wanted me to wear black, stiff, uncomfortable dress shoes, and he wanted me to shine them every Saturday.

Because of the pernicious influence my grandparents held over my wardrobe, I spent the impressionable days of my youth dressed like a refugee from "Revenge of the Nerds." Rarely was I permitted to go shopping by myself. I needed a guardian to protect me from making unwise purchases.

But one day, back when I was in the 11th grade at Landon High School in Jacksonville, my grandparents slipped up. I got to go shopping alone, and I bought some Ivy League chino slacks with a belt in the back — charcoal gray — a thin white belt, a pink dress shirt and a pair of white bucks.

The shoes were the best part. They were just like the ones Pat Boone wore. I was proud of them, especially after several weeks of wear had given them the dull, streaked, gray-dirty look much preferred by my peer group in the mid-1950s.

At last, I was riding the crest of a fad, instead of dressing like a hopeless misfit. More weeks went by, and my white buck shoes were really getting ripe. In fact, to my young eyes, those grimy shoes were perfect.

I woke up one morning and reached under the bed for my shoes and they weren't there. I looked in the closet, and then out in the hall. I didn't remember leaving them in the den, but I checked anyway.

There was noise from the kitchen. My beloved grandfather was sitting at the kitchen table with a cup of coffee, saucered and blowed. Next to his coffee cup, shining gleaming white, still a bit chalky from the liquid shoe polish my grandfather had carefully applied, were my beloved white bucks.

There was a lump in my throat. I tried to speak, but I couldn't find the words. My grandpa looked up and said: "I saw these shoes were pretty dirty, so I polished 'em for you."

Forlorn, I took the shoes out in the back yard and halfheartedly smeared some dirt on them. But the dirt just sat on top of the chalky white polish and it was obvious the dirt was not ground in and a part of the shoe the way it was s'posed to be.

They soon went to the back of the closet and I went back to the black wing-tips my grandparents had picked out for me.

"Now that's a good-looking pair of shoes," my grandfather said with satisfaction. "I never saw what you saw in those ole white ones."

Air-conditioning is No Longer Just for Pantywaists

Back when I was growing up in Jacksonville, it was many moons before I lived in an air-conditioned home. Actually, I was in the first of my three sophomore years at Jacksonville University before my family moved into an air-conditioned domicile.

I owned some pretty snazzy cars when I was a teenager, including a white and gold '57 Mercury and a couple of Chevy Impalas. None were air-conditioned. My first car with that now-necessary add-on was a 1963 Chevy I bought when I was a second lieutenant defending Colorado Springs from communist aggression.

Heck, right now, I'd sooner buy a car that had no engine than one with no air-conditioner.

I have experienced some pretty amazing extremes of weather, from the 69 below zero in a 40-knot wind I once endured on the Greenland icecap to the time I spent a day in a Mexican village across the border from Presidio, Texas, and the mercury was holding steady at 110.

So I tend to be pretty philosophical weather-wise, and am usually content to take what Mother Nature gives me.

My uncomplaining nature (I NEVER whine!) was put to a severe test this Memorial Day when the home air-conditioner went on the fritz. Despite opening all the windows and turning the ceiling fans on to high, the house never would cool down.

It was so miserable that I made excuses to go for drives, just so I could bask in the cool air in the cab of my pick-up truck. I dropped in a couple of bars for draft beers in icy mugs.

I have to confess, I didn't handle the deprivation very well.

And it set me to thinking about how tough I was as a kid, playing baseball in the blazing sun all afternoon and sleeping that night in a bedroom cooled only by a small oscillating fan.

The nice thing about my boyhood homes is that they were shaded by large oak trees and they were built with temperature control in mind. High ceilings and breezy hallways and porches were important parts of the architecture. I remember a lot of times we slept on screened porches or the kids would be allowed to pitch tents in the back yard.

There was always a lot of iced tea in the refrigerator and we kept large bags of crushed ice in the freezer. A drive-in restaurant nearby made cherry limeades with shaved ice. Vendors at Jacksonville Beach did a land-office business selling snow cones. Life was good.

When I would go to visit South Florida relatives, the homes were large and had breezeways. The floors were terrazzo — polished marble chips set in concrete — and I remember how cool it was to the touch. You could lie on the floor with a coloring book, a stack of comics and your portable and the terrazzo actually felt cold.

I would put in workdays at my grandfather's furniture store. He sold fans, and if the day was especially hot, he would open the front and back doors to the store and turn on all the fans. The wind tunnel effect created was sometimes enough to cause papers to fly around the room.

My grandpa, an old Georgia Cracker who spent many a hot, dusty day plowing fields looking up the south end of a northbound mule, would be contemptuous of my current inability to handle a little discomfort.

Air-conditioning, he snorted, was for pantywaists, and it was certainly a huge waste of money.

Since we never experienced air-conditioning except when visiting the local icehouse or when going to the Florida Theater down on Forsyth Street, which advertised "REFRIGERATED AIR" on its marquee, we never knew what we were missing.

There was no complaining, even when the sun blazed so hot that ladies in spike heels were sinking down in the asphalt on city streets.

I went barefoot so much that I could walk across near-molten streets and sidewalks without having to skip real fast to the shade.

Schools weren't air-conditioned either, and anyone who advocated spending tax money on such frills would have been strung up. And the heat was always the worst on the closing days of the term when you really didn't want to be in class anyway.

Everybody talks about growth management, but managed growth is, after all, only a more acceptable form of growth. I have a proposal that separates the contenders from the pretenders growth-management-wise.

I advocate outlawing mosquito control and air-conditioning statewide. Then we would find out who REALLY wants to live here.

I used to think I was one of the ones who would tough it out. After getting bit by an angry horde of mosquitoes on the golf course a couple of months ago and then enduring the great air-conditioning brown-out at the ole homestead last week, I'm not quite as confident.

I'm a mere shell of my former self, and all I used to be was a mere shell.

A Royal Mess
on 'Face the Base'

Our little base in Greenland was buzzing with excitement. A member of the Danish royal family, a prince by trade, was visiting our gallant American fighting men and Danish civilian workers at Sondrestrom, garden spot of the northland.

We made our little permafrost heaven spic and span for the princely tour, but some of us began to notice that the Danish civil servants were even more blase and complacent than usual. Discreet inquiries disclosed that our royal guest was the black sheep of the royal family.

The prince was getting a little long in the tooth and had settled into a life of alcohol and indolence after he was quietly but decisively removed from any hope of succession to the crown.

I was the manager of the Sondy Broadcast System, with a 24 hour, seven day a week radio schedule and 66 hours of television offerings, including my top rated show: "Twelve O'Clock High." All the TV shows were on film except for a brief live news show we produced at six each evening.

When the prince heard that we had a live television newscast, he hoisted his glass and issued a royal decree that he would be our guest star. Even though my radio-TV station was only a 10 minute drive from the Officer's Club, the prince managed to be late. Shortly after six, he swept into the studio and he walked straight to his assigned chair and sat staring straight ahead as a technician pinned a small microphone to his lapel.

That done, I took my seat and the camera, our only one, was turned on. Sondy's version of Face The Base, or maybe Press The Meat, was on the air and cooking. I'm told by my colleagues that I did a sterling job of introducing my guest, at no time betraying the fact that I knew nothing about him except the scurrilous gossip of his countrymen.

One of the things I hadn't known until too late was that the prince wasn't comfortable using English, and three of the four Danish words I knew weren't permitted on the air. The Prince and I were at a contretemps — and in desperate need of an interpreter.

Precious seconds — seemed like hours — of dead air elapsed as the prince and I smiled dumbly into the camera.

I tried to look cool as I grabbed a nearby folding chair and passed it from my left hand to my right hand behind me, placing it next to the seat occupied by my semi-stupefied guest prince.

Our station janitor, a bilingual Danish civilian named Erling, was leaning on his broom as he watched this royal mess. I motioned to Erling to come and sit on the folding chair I had so cleverly interposed between my perch and the prince. The prince looked momentarily discomfited when he saw Erling, who was wearing a grimy, one piece jumpsuit and filthy, scuffed brogans.

But my interpreter was a trooper and he did his best, despite the fact that he was having a bit of trouble understanding the prince, who mumbled a lot. In a fit of petulance, the prince finally told his gracious host and interpreter to move aside while he issued a personal message to his subjects.

He delivered a 45 minute monologue which I'm told covered in detail the nuances of the American-Danish treaties on Greenland, Denmark's continued commitment to NATO, a rehash of European politics before and after World War II and a paean to the virtues of Carlsberg and Tuborg beers. But I can't swear to that.

The prince then made his ramrod straight way back to the O Club bar, while I rushed to the station refrigerator and popped a top with my loyal crew.

The biggest beneficiary of the entire fiasco was Erling, who was looked upon by his countrymen as a television celebrity from that day forward, and a rumor surfaced that a certain lady — employed at the airline terminal on the Danish side of the runway — who previously had rejected Erling's rough hewn advances suddenly decided he was her Prince Charming.

John in Air Force uniform.

Bless the Keepers of the Children

A children's hospital is a wonderful and terrible place. Amid all the happy thoughts racing through my mind this week as I prepare to go to Texas for my daughter Ginger's high school graduation is an uncertain week in 1967 when she had to go to Seattle Children's Hospital.

My infant daughter had developed a large lump, an abscess, behind her right ear. The doctor was calm and reassuring, but said it might be best if the lump were lanced in a hospital rather than in his office.

The minor operation was done the same day we had Ginger admitted to the hospital and it wasn't long before I was allowed to go into her hospital room to see that everything was okay. My happiness at the success of the operation was clouded by the pitiful sight of my baby lying there with her arms in a specially designed gown which had boards in the sleeves.

The nurse in charge of that floor came by to assure me that Ginger was fine and that the boards in the sleeves of the tiny hospital gown were for a good purpose. The special gown kept the little tyke from poking her tiny, pink figures into the stitched incision behind her ear.

Intellectually, I recognized the need for such protection but my heart was near the melting point every time I looked at Ginger. She would flap her little board arms and her eyes seemed to be pleading with me to pick her up and take her home.

Thank goodness for hospital rules and thank goodness there are nurses courageous and compassionate enough to break them.

Children's Hospital had a very strict 8:30 p.m. closing of visiting hours, and that meant parents, too.

But the head nurse winked and said I could stay quietly in Ginger's room for another hour, or at least until the nurses had finished their mandatory routines that went with the ending of visiting hours.

When she came back to tell me that time was up and I definitely would have to leave, we stood in the hall outside of Ginger's room and conversed in a whisper. I found out she had been working at the children's hospital for almost 12 years.

How, I asked with a lump in my throat, can a person work for 12 years in a place where children are in pain and where little baby girls feebly wave the clunky boards stiffening their arms and whine for daddy to take them home? What reserves can we draw on that would enable us to deal day after day with the sorrow of broken little innocents.

"Follow me," the nurse whispered, and we turned left down a corridor and went almost to the end of the hall. We stopped at a room where the door was cracked open and I could see faintly a small form under an oxygen tent.

"Two years old . . . There are 32 cigarette burns on her body. Her father did it." The nurse's voice broke and went up in pitch on the last sentence. It was too much for me. It's hard to say which of us caused the other to start sobbing.

In a darkened hall of a large hospital after closing hours, the tough Air Force captain and the gritty veteran chief nurse held each other tightly and cried for the children. And for ourselves.

The Big Payoff:
a Love Story

It was 1975, and I had made my way back to Florida after a few months on the road, picking up a freelance job here and there and sometimes living off the generosity of friends and relatives.

My path had traced and retraced itself across Texas, up to Kansas City for a week, then down to Louisiana, over to Georgia and then back to Jacksonville, before I finally found a job to replace the one I had thrown away in a fit of anger in Dallas the year before.

I owed about $7,000 to assorted department stores, banks, oil companies and a credit union, and it was one of the happiest times in my life. I long ago had shredded every credit card I owned, but the accumulated debt sat there, unsatisfied, waiting for my decision to quit bumming around and do my part for the economy.

I was in no hurry.

The department stores and oil companies were getting nasty, so I made up my mind that someday, whenever I had enough cash, they would be paid last. The bank, which was holding the paper on my Chevy, was patient because the vice president who had made the loan was a friend who knew that I was the kind who would never duck out on a debt.

The Dallas Teachers Credit Union — ahh, that's the subject of this story.

The account manager who was given my overdue bill of about $800 to handle was a Mrs. Geyer, who would occasionally call or write with motherly lectures about the virtues of thrift and the need to maintain a spotless credit history.

I was so impressed that the credit union had given me a real person, my very own, to deal with instead of the cold, computerized notices of the department store and gasoline bureaucrats, that I decided to strike up a special relationship with Mrs. Geyer.

It all started with a letter I wrote stating that Mrs. Geyer had called me so many times, had written so many letters and handled so many change of address forms for my overdue account, that I was beginning to fall in love with her.

For months, even after I landed a job and was able to make halting, part payments on the debt, I would mail holiday greetings to Mrs. Geyer for Valentines, Christmas, St. Patrick's Day, and such.

If I had no money to include, I would write her a poem, sometimes humorous on the theme of being broke but in love, and sometimes in mock seriousness. If I would move, I would occasionally call personally to give her my new address and phone number and tell her if a pay raise was in the works soon.

She would tsk! and counsel me on the need to be more responsible. I would promise to do better.

By 1976, I was drawing crude representations of hearts or flowers around the borders of my poems, which became even more syrupy and confident of requited love as my outstanding balance sank below the $400 mark.

At last the big day came. Clutching proceeds from a large bonus check from my job, I drove to Dallas and walked in, unannounced, to the main office of the Dallas Teachers Credit Union. I asked, perchance, where would be the desk of one Mrs. Geyer?

I was pointed to a desk in the back of the office where a gray haired, matronly Mrs. Geyer had her nose buried in the file folder of some other financial miscreant, obviously one who never had declared his love for the credit union's bad debt specialist.

I had barely introduced myself when she stood up, clasped her hands together and shrieked: "It's HIM!!" Other office workers ran over to see what had come over the mild mannered Mrs. Geyer. She stammered: "It's . . . It's him. The one I told you about. It's that Carter fellow!"

I plunked down the $354.31, or whatever it was, in cash down to the penny. Mrs. Geyer scooped it up lovingly and turned to her file cabinet to retrieve my folder, which was the thickest one in the drawer. Between the manila covers was every shred of correspondence I had sent — the cards, the amateurish drawings and the love poems of our nearly two years of contact.

She triumphantly handed me a receipt and then the entire office moved into the employee lounge where we celebrated the return of the prodigal son with coffee and doughnuts. There was much handshaking and laughter filled the room.

And Mrs. Geyer leaned over, gave my arm a squeeze and said: "I never doubted you, Mr. Carter. I knew that you wouldn't let me down."

Squirrels: Furry Friends or Tasty Treats?

There were letters and phone calls from those who loathe the little vermin and from some who think of them as best friend of Bullwinkle Moose.

I believe I am uniquely qualified to understand the reasoning on both sides of this argument. For, in my jug-eared, southern-fried lifetime, I have been both messenger of doom and trusted friend to the perky little fellas.

I have been both their worst nightmare and most generous benefactor.

Let me take you back to this week in the year 1950, when I awoke to find a fascinating present for me on my 10th birthday. My grandfather felt I was responsible enough to possess my very own "squirrel fun."

It was a Savage over-and-under with a single shot .22 caliber on top and a single shot .410 shotgun on the bottom.

The gift was followed quickly by a visit to a Georgia farm, where I was given an intensive course in safety, such as how to handle the rifle when climbing a fence, cleaning and storing it and how to quickly thumb down to the .410 shotgun barrel if you missed your target with the .22!

A few days later, I was given my first mission. "I'm hongry, son," my grandpa drawled. "Why don't you run out there in the woods and get us a mess of squirrel."

It wasn't long before I returned with seven fine squirrels tied to my belt. My grandfather showed me how to skin them, cut them in pieces, roll 'em in flour, pan fry, then raise gravy. That was his favorite meal, though for a change of pace he sometimes threw squirrel meat into his Brunswick stew.

After I left home, I stopped hunting and one day gave that trusty, straight-shooting Savage over-and-under away. For one reason or another, I have never shot anything but a paper target since.

The skills my grandfather imparted did help me earn a markmanship medal while in the service, and I was proud of that.

Today, I am the trusted protector and friend of the noble squirrel. Every day, I feed a loyal group of six bushy-tailed little scamps in our backyard. I wouldn't think of harming a single hair on their furry little bodies.

In fact, the recent loss of my best little pet squirrel, Ralph, is still with me. She was getting older and more decrepit each day, and it was harder for her to compete with the younger squirrels.

I hope she died of a dignified old age, though it could be she perished under the wheels of a car.

You've probably noticed by now that I describe Ralph as "she" and that's true. We named her before we ever got a good look at her undercarriage.

Our second clue was the day Ralph came strolling through the yard carrying a tiny baby squirrel around her neck and acting very motherly.

Ralph didn't care what we called her, as long as the supply of roasted peanuts, Brazil nuts and sunflower seeds held out.

We gravitated toward Ralph because it was easy to identify her. She had only one eye. Later, we knew it was her because of her sweet and gentle nature.

She would walk up and put one of her hands on yours as she gently took a nut from your fingers.

She has now gone on to join the choir invisible, but there may be a replacement in the making. There is a small female we believe was the little tyke Ralph was carrying that day.

We have named her "Ralphette" and now she is making the same tentative, meek little steps toward us each day and likely soon will be hand fed as her mother was.

Like some critics, we know intellectually they are just rats with bushy tails, but emotionally they have squirreled their way into our hearts. We get a daily vaudeville show in our backyard and all it costs us is peanuts.

Life is good.

He's Sitting Pretty
on the St. Johns

Everyone needs a retreat, someplace they can repair to when solitude is desired, or in my case, required.

The place that I enjoy the most is the St. Johns River, a waterway which I once took for granted. Now I feel very protective of it.

Since joining The News-Journal papers back in 1976, I have been one of the most avid readers of the excellent reports on the river penned by our environmental writers — Don Lindley, then Mary McLachlin and now Jim Hartman.

My idea of a perfect getaway day is to drive to Volusia Landing, head north to the South Moon Fish Camp, rent a boat with a six horse power kicker on it and move slowly out into the channel of what I believe is the greatest river in the World.

I can't tell an egret from a heron, or a box turtle from a gopher, but I enjoy the sights and sounds of the St. Johns and its tributaries. My favorite side trip is the loop of Blue Creek which runs on the Lake County side from near the South Moon camp to the mouth of Lake George.

Massive alligators roll off logs and rows of turtles sun themselves on limbs of trees stretched horizontally across the water from the shady shore. Large blue-gray birds with feathery gray "beards" stand motionless in the shallows, their spearlike beaks poised to strike.

I tie the boat up to a dead tree and reach down to the baitbucket to trap one of the 50 or so crickets I bought at the fish camp. I bait up and pitch the wiggly little critter over to the base of a stump or let the current carry it against a submerged fallen tree.

If I'm lucky a near two pound bluegill will inhale that sucker and I'll drag him out from under a stump and into my livewell. Most likely, a bunch of little stumpknockers or redeyes will steal my bait.

No matter what happens, I'm sitting pretty in the middle of some of the most beautiful country Florida has to offer, accompanied by a Thermos full of iced tea and a brown bag filled with roast beef sandwiches and two packs of Tom's malt crackers.

After gliding through the creek and maybe fishing that little clump of pilings near the entrance to Lake George, I lean back and watch a glorious sunset before aiming the little boat back to camp. The livewell usually contains about a dozen bluegill or shellcracker, and maybe even a catfish.

If I feel up to cleaning them, there'll be fresh fish on the table that night. If I'm real lazy, and I usually am, I give them away to one of the families renting a cabin by the river. Once in a while, I have the satisfaction of "making a mess" of fish for dinner for some visitor who didn't do so well that day and had been considering a drive to a nearby restaurant.

I'm pretty selfish about the St. Johns, and get downright edgy if I hear too much talk about anyone damaging it any worse than it has been. I owe quite a bit to Don, Mary and Jim, because they're willing to travel to the headwaters, attend a bunch of boring meetings in places like Palatka and even, gulp, read a dreaded environmental impact statement in order to keep the river's plight before the public.

I've never been to a headwaters. I hate meetings. I hope to go through the rest of my life without ever having to read an environmental impact statement. But I do love that river, and if you're one of those trying to save it, count me a friend.

But if you're one of the greedheads who is doing anything to threaten the St. Johns in any way, then you've got on the fightin' side of me.

School Was the Tie that Confined

Edna Conatser, bless her heart, was a lady of refinement and dedication to the art/science of education. Possessor of a Vanderbilt degree and a sonorous voice that would make William F. Buckley Jr. envious, Mrs. Conatser was a stylishly stout force to be reckoned with at Beulah Beal Elementary School in Jacksonville during the 1940s.

She was one of two fifth grade teachers, but it seemed that she dominated the school and set the tone and agenda for it. Possibly she was more powerful than the principal and she led the way through sheer force of will and intellect.

I describe her in such detail only to set up the chilling brace of facts I'm about to relay to you.

1. I was a happy go lucky little kid at Beulah Beal who was making good grades without actually doing much schoolwork until I reached the fifth grade and was assigned to the classroom of you know who.

2. Edna Conatser rented the upstairs apartment from my folks and chatted with them (usually about my progress in school) practically every day! As you can imagine, I was doomed.

Having your teacher living upstairs was a definite liability. I never could lie and say I had no homework assigned. It was too easy for my grandparents to holler up the stairwell and check it out. Was there any hope of hiding the shameful fact I had been forced to stand out in the hall for 30 minutes because I had disrupted the class by talking, throwing paper airplanes or making cootie-catchers? Guess.

115

So when I left the halls of Beulah Beal and headed for eighth grade adventures at Kirby-Smith Junior High, I was elated at the thought that my every mistake and misdemeanor would not be reported to my folks by Agent Conatser each night.

After my first day at the new school, Mrs. Conatser and my grandparents gathered 'round to ask who my teachers were. When I mentioned that my homeroom teacher was Mrs. Hunt, Edna Conatser beamed. She assured my grandparents that there would be little opportunity for me to goof off in junior high.

My homeroom teacher, it turned out, was a dear friend and confidante of our upstairs boarder. The intelligence reports on my conduct and educability continued for another year and a half, when we moved over to the southside.

Edna Conatser, as powerful and resourceful as she was in the Springfield and Brentwood neighborhood schools, was unable to reach me at Landon Junior-Senior High. I thought I was home free.

That is, until my Uncle Frank came for a visit a few days later and told my grandparents the news. "Guess what?" Frank Carter reported, "my old football coach at Jackson, Mike Houser, is the assistant principal at Landon. He said Johnny was sent down to his office yesterday for talking in class."

School certainly was an education for me.

Stepparents Know Love Isn't a Matter of Biology

Stepfathers and stepmothers get a lot of bad press. Gosh, even the Disney movies feature evil stepmothers and cruel stepfathers. According to the old country saying, there's nothing worse than to be "treated like a stepchild."

That's a shame, because there's an awful lot of love and longing going on in this crazy world between lucky kids and affectionate stepparents.

I stood beside my mother last Monday during funeral services for one of the kindest, dearest and most dependable men I've ever known — Edd Reese Jr. He was my stepfather, but the obituary printed last week in the Broward County edition of the Miami Herald listed me as his son.

That's a compliment I accept gratefully. He has been such an important part of my mom's life and my life for nearly four decades that I might as well be Edd Reese III instead of John David Carter.

I'm prejudiced in favor of people with Edd's strong points. When I examine the lives of the few men who have been strong role models in my life, the ones I admire the most, it seems they all were shy several years of formal book learnin' but had a bumper crop of common sense and countrified humor.

Edd Reese loved me and wanted me to consider myself part of his family a long time before I caught on that he did. He was the strong silent type, an outdoorsman with remarkable hunting and fishing skills who didn't cotton much to sentimentality.

But he was never too macho to do housework, cuddle up with the most spoiled poodle dog on this planet or tease little jug-eared kids like me and my late brother.

I'm a stepfather myself now, and I catch myself reaching out to those young'uns the same way Edd hinted and insinuated himself into my life. I learned how to be a stepfather by following Edd's example, and though I sometimes fail, most of the time I think I'm doing pretty good.

Marriages don't seem to last in these troubled times and we see more stepdaddies and stepmommies created each day. Most of them want to do the right thing and would play a larger role in the lives of the stepkids if they were encouraged. You're being cheated out of a lot if you confuse mere biology with true love.

Cinderella's cruel stepmother is the exception, not the rule. I know several ladies who treat their husband's progeny from a previous marriage with great grace and humor. And yes, love. And I can say the same for several stepdads I know. For all of you longsuffering and loving surrogate moms and dads out there, here's a Sunday Punch salute.

Have you hugged your stepfather today? I haven't, but I sure would if I could . . .

When the Feeling
Was Still Fresh

1957 — What a year! It was the year I was honorably rolled out of public high school, which I hated, and enrolled in college, which I enjoyed too much. But mostly, 1957 was the greatest year in the history of the American automobile. Those Chevys, Fords, Plymouths, Pontiacs and, yes, my beloved white Mercury with the gold inserts along the top of the fenders still shine in my mind as the greatest chariots ever.

It's difficult to get excited about cars these post-pseudo-oil-crisis days — these pathetic little buggies choked down with bogus emission control devices. The throaty roar of a 300 horsepower. Chevy engine firing exhaust through a glasspack muffler was the sound of the '50s.

Those were cars a teenager could get fired up about. Every traffic light was a challenge. Hormones raging and hearts racing, we would signal to the Ford or Plymouth next to us: "Wanna drag?"

Though I was proud of my Merc, most everyone agreed that the '57 Pontiac was the fastest jackrabbit on wheels for the first 50 yards. The guys who ran Pontiacs in the days when Jacksonville's now crowded Fort Caroline Road and Bowden Road were considered out in the country went through tires like popcorn.

After taking your steady to the Toot'n Tell'm Drive In, it was considered good form to lay a trail of smoking rubber on the driveway to the street. Sure, it was dangerous. Yes, it was stupid. But what the hell . . . we didn't do drugs. Even though we dressed like hoods, who turned up collars and held a cigarette tucked wetly and inexpertly in the half sneer that we adopted as our semi-official expression, most of us were pretty harmless and naive.

The most amazing evidence that we were mere babes in the woods was our firm conviction that the success of cars running the races at Daytona had even a remote connection to the quality of the drag racing machine we owned. No one in their right mind today believes that anyone could walk into a car dealer's showroom and buy a Ford that will put you fender to fender with Bill Elliott.

My young friends believed with all their hearts that the '57 Pontiac that Cotton Owens drove to victory on the old beach-road course here was just like the ones in the showroom. And the Chevy owners made excuses about Johnny Beauchamp's second place finish.

Most of the arguing was going on between the Pontiac and Chevy owners. I was pretty well satisfied to hear that Fonty Flock finished third in his '57 Mercury.

And in that most romantic of internal combustion years, NASCAR launched a policy to de-emphasize the link between the performance of cars on the track and their marketability at the dealerships. Not that the car manufacturers or auto racing kingpins pursued the noncommercialization goal very seriously, but the sport eventually outgrew the silly boasts of 16 year olds who had just acquired a driver's license. It became a big business.

Like Pickett's charge at Gettysburg, 1957 seems to me the high water mark of my generation's love affair with wheels. I've never owned another car that made me as happy as that powerful Merc, and don't expect I ever will.

After then, the newness kinda wore off. We got too smart for our britches. So many distractions started getting in the way. The romance died.

Was It Aliens? or the
Magic of a Woman?

'Til now, I always thought "Invasion of the Body Snatchers" a charming fiction. The thought of aliens taking our friends and relatives while replacing them with clones grown from pods used to be outlandish to me.

Pure science fiction.

Science fiction is now science fact. I have strong suspicions my son David is a pod person. Some alien force has replaced the lackadaisical, irresponsible son I once knew.

How do I know this? Hah! Glad you asked. Just a few days ago, I received a formal thank-you note from David.

Maybe not a big deal to those of you in normal families, but this is an event off the seismic scale in the shattered Carter household. We, umm, aren't real strong on etiquette. Carters have trouble figuring out which one is the salad fork and we wonder why you can't drink out of the finger bowl.

Jelly glasses do real good for wine or iced tea, either one, and the most uptown thank-you note we ever wrote was scribbled on a Big Chief tablet.

David Alan Carter was so laid back he was dern near comatose. He seemed content living a placid life in one of the prettiest parts of the nation, the redwood country up in Eureka, California.

The only way we could get him to communicate with the rest of the family most times is on computer via the Internet, where he spends a

121

large number of his waking hours.

So I open this fancy little envelope and pull out a small card emblazoned "With Special Thanks." Inside, in David's own handwriting — I had always wondered what his handwriting actually looked like — was a message thanking me for the present I gave him Christmas Day.

David has never acted like that in all his 31 years. Yep, that's a 3 and a 1. Something mid-life-changing has happened to my son and heir, or else the pod people snagged him and sent in a clone.

And the thank-you note isn't the only sign.

David wears nicer clothes, cuts his hair, drives a new car, goes on hikes in the woods, takes pictures of the breathtaking California coast, drinks cappuccino, has enrolled in a degree program at the College of the Redwoods and broadened his interest in music from a previous steady diet of Zappa and cyberpunk.

I was slow to pick up on the reasons, but all you women readers have already guessed. Sorry guys, but you are like me and haven't yet figured out the genesis of David's radical makeover.

What happened is that David has met a vision of loveliness and intends to marry her next July. I was always skeptical about the power of women over men until I witnessed this miraculous transformation. If there ever was a prime exhibit for the positive effects of womanhood, here it is.

I just met the object of David's affections — my future daughter-in-law — and I, too, am smitten by her beauty, charm and temperament. Her name is BunE, and yep that is a capital E. It is a Korean name which we have shortened to sound like "Boone" and she works for the admissions office at Humboldt State University.

Yeah, I forgot to mention she's smart, too.

David is so flat et up with BunE that he spends most all of his time waxing eloquent about her. And this is a guy who used to wouldn't even wax his car.

I'm trying to save a little money and vacation time to fly out to California for the nuptials. They showed me a nifty picture and also a videotape of the cliff overlooking the Pacific where they plan to tie the knot.

It looks like something out of a travelog, with sea lions playing in the water, swimming around huge outcroppings of rock in the surf.

Every woman I have told this to has had the same reaction. Why am I surprised? This, they say, is the civilizing effect women have over all men.

The most interested observers of this metamorphosis of David from frog to prince are his sisters Karen and Ginger. They were beginning to despair that their stinky ole brother was ever gonna mend his ways.

But even at a young age, they were aware of the superior moral position held by females and the grungy underclass of males.

The girls loved to jump rope when they were little tykes. I've always remembered their favorite jump rope rhyme. Even then Karen and Ginger were aware of the proper order of things, as they chanted:

Boys go to Jupiter

To get more stupider

Girls go to Mars

To eat candy bars

I wonder if those body snatchers who spirited away my number one son came from Jupiter? That would be poetic justice in a way. But I'm in a win-win situation here. It looks like I have done more than just gained a daughter-in-law. Looks like I also get a new, improved 1995 V-8 David.

Cats are number one.

Feline-ious Act:
Cats Steal Hearts

Eat your heart out, Lassie. Tell Old Yeller to suck an egg. Snoopy can go play in traffic.

The market research geniuses have finally figured out what Morris, Heathcliff and Garfield have known for years. Cats are number one.

There are now 56.2 million felines in America, outnumbering canines by almost 5 million. The independent, easy-to-care-for cat is the pet of the '80s and the popular choice of singles and small families who don't want to be tied down to the ole homestead, the geniuses say.

Now I have nothing against dogs. Some of them are as intelligent as cats. And those of us who are cat people shouldn't be disrespectful to those who are dog people.

I am a former dog person, and as a child I romped through the Springfield section of Jacksonville with Rusty, my overly faithful cocker spaniel. And far be it from me to be critical of poodles, since my dear sainted mother owns the most spoiled example of that breed which ever lived.

If you get the feeling I'm weasel-wording all this because I don't want to cross my Mom and her precious pooch Bridget, well, maybe so. If some crude, thoughtless person sends her a copy of this column, I've got a helluva lot of explaining to do.

I am a cat person three times over, and my current owners are Mama Cat, Twinkle and Buford. Twinkle is Mama Cat's daughter and

125

Buford is an orphan we took into our home Christmas night when he was but a shivering, flea-infested insignificant ball of black and white fluff.

The older cats, both calicos, aren't exactly thrilled with the kittenish antics of Buford and they are very pleased that he is growing up and becoming calmer.

Poor Buford went around for weeks with a clawed nose because he decided to frolic too close to the sleeping Mama Cat one day. She batted him a good one and he kept his place for at least, say, an hour.

The attention span of a kitten is not significantly longer than that of a second grader.

Cats usually require less care and expense than dogs, and they add a touch of elegance to the decor. Why put up with a slobbering, yelping and leaping creature every time you come home? Cats simply eye you imperiously as if to say: "Oh, it's you again."

Dogs have masters. Cats are masters. There's a difference.

The swing toward the feline end of the pet spectrum is big business. Cat food sales have more than doubled since 1979 and now total $2 billion per year. I don't want to make any wild claims about where that puts kitties in the popularity parade, but I report without malice or editorializing that cat food out sold baby food last year.

The breakdown is 1.25 billion pounds of moist cat food and 1 billion pounds of dry. And, ahem, cat owners purchased more that a million tons of cat litter.

And that just scratches the surface. Look at the increasing popularity of cat oriented greeting cards, comic strips, T-shirts, children's books and even a smash Broadway play.

That ain't woofin', believe you me.

A Stomach Full of Memories

My goal has always been to simplify my life, but somehow things never end up simple. While growing up, I cheerfully ate okra, grits, spinach, rutabagas, boiled peanuts, bread pudding and Brussels sprouts without knowing they were controversial.

— JC

A Good Meal Makes
for a Happy Cracker

Florida Cracker menfolk love good home cooking, no doubt about it. And we enjoy it at both ends of the food chain, as both consumers and creators.

A Florida Cracker "Alpha Male" takes great pride in his culinary skills and has a few favorite recipes he'll brag on to beat the band. For instance, I make a killer spaghetti sauce, whip up a larrupin' okra and tomato stir-fry and work wonders with speckled perch filets, either fried in a hush-puppy coating or broiled with butter and lime.

A Florida Cracker man is also king of his barbecue grill. When the family comes over, all the grilling is done by the menfolk, who stand around the glowing coals swilling beer and swapping bodacious stories.

All these things are testosterone-based.

Don't make any assumptions based on those traits that Florida Cracker Alpha Males have any interest in day-to-day kitchen work. Routine meals, proper planning and cleanup details are best left to the wimmenfolk.

Our goal is to be the occasional stars of the show, not the ones you depend on for the long haul.

That thought struck me when I was talking to Don, a Lakeland-born buddy, now living in Ormond Beach. His wife, Betty, rules the kitchen, but Don claimed he is the king of the barbecue grill. He commandeers the kitchen from time to time to make one of his special gourmet creations.

By the way, it's a good thing to be on their Christmas list. Every year, Don concocts a batch of his killer barbecue sauce and Betty creates her home-grown Amaretto liqueur, which they give away as presents.

Don told me they were driving through Hazlehurst, Georgia, recently and stopped at a place called "Courson's Country Kitchen."

All the vittles were fresh from the farm and you had your pick of several entrees, side dishes and desserts and iced tea for the princely sum of $5.50 per person. I don't know why the thought of all that pigging out made them think of me (ahem), but Don dropped by The Little Miracle of 6th Street recently to tell me all about it.

He also had to brag about all the neat dishes he prepares, which made me brag right back about my success spatula-wise.

"I've cooked all my life," Don reported, adding that he uses the traditional Cracker cooking method which needs no recipe book, or if a recipe is employed, it is embellished considerably. "I guess you could call me bullheaded. I like to do it my way," he confessed.

I knew exactly what he meant. I speak "bullheaded" like a native.

All regular Sunday Punch readers know that from time to time I have published what I consider noteworthy recipes in this space.

In that tradition, I present a recipe Don gave me for a scrumptious "Peanut Butter Pound Cake."

Here's the deal. Take 2 1/2 sticks of butter and 2 cups of sugar and mix until light yellow. Beat in 6 eggs, one at a time and add one tsp. of vanilla extract.

Slowly beat in 1/2 cup of peanut butter, and it doesn't matter whether it's smooth or crunchy. Sift 2 cups of all-purpose flour, one tsp. of baking soda and 1/4 tsp. of salt together, then add this to the other mixture slowly until well blended. Line a tube pan with wax paper and spoon in batter.

Bake at 350 degrees for 45 minutes, reduce heat to 325 degrees and bake 15 minutes longer, until cake "tests" done. If you like, you can add finely chopped peanuts as a topping.

Here's the fun part. Don stole that recipe fair and square. Actually, he found it in an old cookbook put together by a Junior Women's League in West Georgia. The recipe was donated by the wife of a prosperous peanut farmer in those parts: "Mrs. Jimmy Carter (Rosalynn.)"

Spearheading a One-man Fan Club for Asparagus

When I was just a little jug-eared kid growing up in Jacksonville, I had a few weird food preferences that sorta puzzled my folks.

Like a lot of kids, I would come in from yard work or play and drink milk directly from the bottle, which really ticked off my grandmother. Another thing she thought was strange was that I liked mayonnaise sandwiches.

But what got my grandma really spinning was my obsession for canned asparagus. I loved the stuff, sometimes with a dollop of mayonnaise on top, but sometimes the light green spears were plucked right out of the can as finger-food.

For most of my life, I preferred canned asparagus to the real thing. I liked the soggy consistency of the canned shoots instead of the sometimes stringy fresh veggie. Plus, I don't recall that fresh asparagus was even available in Jacksonville stores when I was growing up.

I love the fresh variety now and it's fairly easy to find at most produce departments. In fact, I have learned to appreciate the fresh kind steamed or in stir-fry dishes. Well, heck, I got to thinking this week about where does asparagus come from, and I assume it ain't from the valley of the Jolly Green Giant.

I used our esteemed News-Journal Internet Services to search out asparagus news and views from across the nation and came up with more than I ever wanted to know.

For instance, one of the first items I found was a recipe for Stir Fried

Moose with Asparagus and Red Peppers in Black Bean Sauce.

Whew! I didn't read it, but I hope the recipe doesn't start with: "First chop up a moose into little strips . . ."

What I did learn is there is a veritable WAR going on out there between two communities competing for the title of "Asparagus Capital of the U.S."

In one corner is Stockton, California, which had its 11th annual Asparagus Festival in April, and the other contender is Shelby, Michigan, which held its 23rd annual festival about a month ago.

Both communities have their spears sharpened for combat, and have the festival "spear-it," and word-pun on the word "spirit" which both use to excess.

This is no small competition. In Stockton, 4,500 volunteers split up into 70 committees that have donated more than $2 million to charity, all in the name of asparagus.

There are many events, such as races, car shows, arts and crafts, but my favorite, of course, has to do with food. In Stockton's "Asparagus Alley," the following treats are vended: Deep-fried Asparagus, Asparagus Pasta, Asparagus Bisque, Asparaberry Shortcake, Asparagus Ice Cream (Whoa! Suddenly the doggoned moose doesn't sound so bad!), Asparagus Nachos with Asparagus Salsa, Asparagus and Beef Sandwiches and Asparaburritos.

Another nice touch. The Stockton public transportation shuttle system is called the "Asparabus."

The Michigan asparagus industry traces its birth back to the Great Chicago fire of 1871. It seems that hundreds of thousands of acres of white pine in Michigan were harvested in the massive effort to rebuild Chicago.

Farmers decided the denuded rolling hills would be ideal for a crop like . . . asparagus! Now there are 500 asparagus growers in the state and 9,700 acres of Oceana County farmland is dedicated to the tender, green shoots.

Asparagus is in the history books, derived from an ancient Greek word referring to all tender shoots of plants. As early as 200 B.C., the Romans issued instructions on how to grow it. In the first century, asparagus was loaded onto fast chariots and taken to the snowline of the Alps to be frozen.

It was kept there six months and then brought back to Rome for the Feast of Epicurus. And you thought Clarence Birdseye invented frozen food, I bet. Asparagus is still an Epicurean delight in Europe, though they lean toward the white and purple stalks rather than the green ones preferred in America.

There you go, Buckarros. Another Sunday Punch food fest, replete with history, nutrition, moose meat and heartwarming reveries of jug-eared days in Jacksonville.

Is this a full service column or what?

Nothing Like Popcorn and Coconut Oil

When I was growing up in Jacksonville, a one-block square of palm trees, sidewalks and park benches was the center of our tiny universe.

It was called Hemming Park, and it was the place where all city buses converged, and you could ride all day on a dime, because transfers were free.

The park was graced by a little cart, where a vendor sold cotton candy, snow cones, popcorn and peanuts parched or boiled.

There's nothing on that list that we didn't like, but the fondest memory was the popcorn, which was served in a way I've never seen since.

The vendor sold popcorn in paper bags, ranging from very small to some as large as a windsock. As he filled each bag, the popcorn man would reach over and pick up a little silver pitcher, with a long narrow spout, kind of like a miniature watering can.

He poured a viscous, steaming potion on the popcorn which made it taste unlike any I've ever had before or since. I had to ask what it was, and he said it was coconut oil.

Well, hell, no one was talking about clogged arteries back in the 1940s, least of all in a place like Jacksonville where all the best cooks laced everything with lard.

You may not believe this, but there is a spirited war of words over the supposed deleterious effects of coconut oil on the human body. Some health watchdog groups have screamed that a box of popcorn laced with coconut oil is like eating "six Big Macs."

134

But apologists say that's hogwash. Others say that even if true, the burden of the system is worth it because of the better taste.

Air popped vs. coconut oil? Sorry, folks, but I vote coconut, and it appears that most moviegoers agree. A 1994 survey shows that seven out of 10 movie concession stands still pop the tasty kernels with coconut oil, on the grounds that any other oil is not worth its salt, which is another nutritional no-no that I won't get into now.

As always, I have worked my head to the bone to come up with some obscure trivia. Did you know that American Indians were the first popcorn vendors?

When Columbus arrived in the West Indies, Indians sold popcorn to his crew. There's no record if they also sold cotton candy, snow cones or boiled peanuts.

The oldest ears of popcorn ever found were discovered in the Bat Cave of west central New Mexico in 1948. The oldest Bat Cave ears are about 5,600 years old.

In tombs on the east coast of Peru, researchers have found grains of popcorn perhaps, 1,000 years old. These grains have been so well-preserved that they will still pop.

In southwestern Utah, a 1,000-year-old popped kernel of popcorn was found in a dry cave inhabited by predecessors of the Pueblo Indians.

And you thought the popcorn you bought at the theater was stale.

According to the popcorn board, the first popcorn machine, probably one not much different from the one which gladdened my childhood at Hemming Park, was invented in 1885 by a man named Charlie Cretors.

The Cretors family is still in the business, and odds are good that you have consumed a product at a theater concession stand that was made in one of their poppers.

Home poppers were first introduced around 1925, and a few years later they were quite the favorite project of kids enrolled in public school shop classes.

But the most remarkable advance in popcornology came in 1945. An inventor named Percy Spencer discovered that corn would pop if exposed to microwave energy.

This led to experiments with other foods and eventually the invention of (applause) the microwave oven. So popping corn was the inspiration for the microwave and many folks still consider it the prime use of a microwave.

Reheating pizza is probably the only other function which might challenge the supremacy of corn-popping, but I vote in favor of the popcorn.

And drench mine in coconut oil, please. Too much ain't enough!

Photo: Mark Lane

John . . . no jumpy tummy here.

Come and Grit'em while They're Good and Hot

Today's topic separates the rans from the also rans, the bees from the wanna bees, the scalawags from the carpetbaggers, the rednecks from the no-necks and the yankees from the damyankees.

Grits.

There. I said it, and I'm glad. I was raised on those wonderful tasty little carbo-loaded calorie bombs, and I consider them more effective even than okra in determining who is and who isn't serious about southern cooking.

I didn't mean for it to, but this column has veered beyond my control into a salute of the great state of South Carolina.

In April, the crossroads hamlet of St. George hosts the World Grits Festival.

It's a grand event, with beauty contests for all age groups, a contest where folks roll around in a tub of grits, a grits-eating contest, parades, concerts, carnivals, dancing and softball tournament. Wellll, kiss my grits!

I wouldn't have known about all the big doin's in St. George if it hadn't been for the kindness of a friend in Ormond Beach, who sent a letter saying she likes grits and included a festival brochure.

I wrote off to the address on the pamphlet and got a whole passel of stuff back from what must be Miz Grits her own self, Nell Bennett. The package contained a videotape of people dunking themselves in a huge tub of grits hoping to win a stereo system (I am not making this

137

up, I saw the tape) and Nell doing a bang-up job as mistress of ceremonies for the grits-eating contest.

"The best grits in the universe are right here in St. George, cooked at Camp Meeting on wood stoves for several hours. Camp Meeting is a week-long gathering ending always on the first Sunday in October. It is a religious meeting and eating, with hundreds of meals being served at each of the 100 tents each day, three times a day," Nell writes.

That last paragraph was in response to my question asking Nell, a recognized expert, where the best grits are served. In fact, if you readers have any nominees, I'd like to hear from you. I'm looking for worthy challengers to the Suwannee Cove Restaurant on the banks of the Suwannee River near Branford, Florida.

A local leader who once wrote a neat song about the joy of grits told me it was Suwannee Cove grits, pure and simple, that inspired him.

By the way, grits are big news in South Carolina. More than 45,000 attended last April's blowout in St. George (pop. 2,000). It all got a big write-up in the Atlanta papers, which made all the folks proud.

I'm always on the lookout for interesting facts about grits, so I stole a few statistics from writer Drew Jubera of the Atlanta Journal-Constitution, who attended this year's World Grits Festival.

Almost everything you've ever heard about grits is true. That's the first thing. They are just as good or just as bad as you always thought they would be. That is a comforting thought in these days when things sometimes are not as advertised.

For instance, South Carolinians eat more grits than anybody else in the world, scarfing down about 14 pounds a year per household. The national average is about one pound per household. About two-thirds of the 103 million pounds of grits sold in the U.S. each year are eaten in the South.

There have been five World Grits Festivals. The idea was hatched by a grits salesman and the owner of the local Piggly Wiggly store after they tried and failed to get a huge 16-ton grits display into the Guiness Book of World Records.

St. George boosters admit they were a trifle ambitious calling their event a "World" festival, but so far no one has contradicted them. It looks like they have a mortal lock on the gritsfest business.

Oh, I can't quit until I tell you that grits is the centerpiece of a Cracker nouvelle cuisine being highly promoted by a grits company.

There are recipes for such culinary treats as Grits Pudding by Maudene Leschinsky of Quinby, South Carolina; the "Y'all Come Back" breakfast by Dell Wanda Gorman of Pine Bluff, Arkansas; Creamy Butterscotch Grits from Nicole Bulley of Columbia, South Carolina. And a brochure has the makins' of Grits and Ham Dinner Quiche, Fried Cheese Party Bites (Honest! I'm not making this up), Jalapeno Cheese Grits and Chili Beef Grits Bake. Personally, I like mine best with a touch of good ole red-eye gravy.

Mouth-watering Salute to the Lowly Hush Puppy

Last Sunday's column on grits got one of my buddies reminiscing about his introduction to Southern cooking. He told me about how he headed south from his Flint, Michigan, home many moons ago as a bright-eyed young swimmer on scholarship at the University of Tennessee.

In the burnt orange dining room of the athletic dorm, he plopped down for his first meal and saw a plate piled high with little fried blobs of various shapes and sizes.

"I thought they were Tater Tots, at least until I bit down into one of them," Bob said.

It was a sink-or-swim introduction to that fine old southern staple: The hush puppy.

A testament to the fact that a southerner will deep-fry anything, the humble hush puppy has been a mainstay of the cuisine since the War for Southern Independence. Or as my Aunt Dovie in Georgia used to call it, the "Late Unpleasantness."

There is even a theory that it originated during the war, when a band of rebels at a campfire used fried cornbread to hush the dogs as a platoon of Yankee soldiers came nearby. But that theory was advanced by Craig Claiborne of the Noo Yawk Times, which I dare say is not the Larousse Gastronomique of Dixie custom and cookery.

(I threw that last part in because I know how much y'all love it when I speak French!)

There are more believable companion theories that though the fried cornmeal was used to quiet dogs, hush puppies were not discovered until just after the war in southern farm kitchens or in Florida Panhandle turpentine camps. The first written reference to this concoction as a hush puppy was not until 1918, according to the Dictionary of Americanisms.

The strangest theory, and one which I personally find unbelievable, is that the first hush puppies were actually fried salamanders, amphibians which in southern slang were known as "water dogs," "water puppies" or "mudpuppies."

I don't believe that for a minute, and I don't think you do either.

Hush puppies are big across the South. In North Carolina, it's common for hush puppies to be served with that region's unique and excellent barbecue. Some of the most famous Tar Heel pups are produced in Lexington at a famous eatery.

In Tennessee, they are a side dish at many of the Volunteer State's fine catfish restaurants. One of those is the Catfish Hotel in Shiloh, which is famous for more than just being a famous battle site during the War of Northern Aggression.

Shiloh is the home of a bodacious hush puppy factory, producing more than a million of the tasty little mealy calorie-bombs per day.

In Mississippi, canny cooks use cayenne to create a mouth-burning little hush puppy known to locals as "Delta Dogs." That sounds pretty good. I'm gonna try that next time I whomp up a batch.

When Kentucky novelist James Still talked about hush puppies a few years back on the National Public Radio show "All Things Considered," the network was swamped with calls and letters asking for his recipe.

You'll be proud to hear that of all the half-truths and outright lies in hush puppy history, Florida leads the pack. Kinda makes you quietly proud, doesn't it?

In the 1950s, the Saturday Evening Post declared the unconquered Florida capital of Tallahassee as the birthplace of hush puppies. The Chamber of Commerce eagerly accepted the accolade, but didn't have a clue as to whether it was true.

Actual-like, the place with a more formidable claim to be called hush puppy heaven is just a few miles south of the state capital. It's a Gulf Coast burg called St. Marks. This esteemed hamlet is the home of Posey's Restaurant, which says right out on its menu that it is the birthplace of the hush puppy.

None dare call it treason, because Posey's founder, a former mayor of St. Marks, may very well have picked up the recipe from one of the Panhandle turpentine camps early in this century.

Perusal of Florida cookbooks reveals a pantheon of modern day hush puppy heroes. There is Shorty Hodges of Cedar Key, saluted for his use of ketchup in the recipe. And not to forget Ruby Lord, the "hush puppy queen" of the annual seafood festival in Grant, down in Brevard County, and Jane Burbank, member of a Fernandina Beach fishing family, who once fried 2,000 pups for a town supper.

I close with a comment on hush puppies from none other than Marjorie Kinnan Rawlings, of "Cross Creek" and "The Yearling" fame. She termed hush puppies *"a concomitant of the hunt,"* going on to explain that *"fresh-caught fish without hush puppies are as a man without a woman."*

Amen, Sister Marjorie, Amen.

Georgian to Celebrate Vidalia Onions

If you know your onions, you'll watch your May calendar for two big festivals in Georgia.

My original plan was to write that at last they've come up with a weekend so good it'll bring tears to your eyes, but that line would offend the good folks in Vidalia and thereabouts who pride themselves on the sweetness and non-lachrymose qualities of their product.

The product being honored May 11-12 in Glennville and May 17-19 in Vidalia is the noble onion, which in the 1930s was named for Vidalia. At this point I would like to declare a conflict-of-interest, in that my Georgia kin in the Baxley and Surrency area farm in one of the counties, Appling by name, are legally permitted to market their onions with the Vidalia name.

But because my uncles, aunts and cousins mainly made their name in the sweet potato biz, I can brag on these onions without too much of a corrupting influence.

This week I got a whole bunch of neat onion-related lore from Melody Hyde of the Vidalia Onion Committee. The committee has to be ever alert to spot those who would fob off bitter, tears-in-your-eyes onions grown many miles from the 20 counties licensed to carry the name as gen-yoo-wine Vidalias.

They report those who misuse the name, and Georgia agriculture officials are seeking federal protection for the product. This may sound like small potatoes to you, but Vidalias are a $30 million cash crop.

143

That's the sweet smell of success.

About 70 percent of the crop is sold in supermarkets, and the remaining 30 percent is purveyed by mail order and in roadside stands. Vidalia onions have a higher water and sugar content than most, so they bruise easily and must be stored with care.

They can be frozen, but some people take the trouble to wrap each one in aluminum foil and keep them in the refrigerator. Another method recommended by the committee is to place the onions in the legs of old pantyhose, tying a knot between each onion.

Melody says the big suspense this year is if anyone can be found to beat the record set by a 12-year-old young'un last year. He ate 10 raw Vidalias in five minutes. That may not sound like many, but maybe you'd be more impressed if you tried it.

She said onions were considered sacred by the ancient Egyptians and were as valuable as gold in the Middle Ages. Because of their high Vitamin C content (as much as an orange and twice as much as an apple), they were carried aboard ships to prevent scurvy.

This was a long time before the invention of the breath mint, and about the time some sailors were mistaking manatees for mermaids.

The column gets a little strange here, folks, but you knew it would, didn't you? One of the winning festival recipes in 1989 was a drink, dubbed the "Yumion Rumion." The formula is "one Vidalia onion, to taste, 6 ounces of rum, three teaspoons of sugar and 16 ounces of frozen limeade." (I'm not making this up.)

"Chop onion and place in blender with rum and limeade. Turn on for two minutes. Add ice and sugar until blender is full. Serves 5 or 6."

Whoa! I'm not going to be too critical until I've tried it, but this recipe has the potential to make the Sunday Punch booze Hall of Fame, right next to my "Pea-tini" recipe from the Athens, Texas, Black-Eyed Pea Festival. (It's a dry martini topped with a black-eyed pea.)

Melody says not all of the onion recipes are like that. For instance she gave me a high-toned one called "Confetti Salad," created by the American Festival Cafe in Rockefeller Plaza, Noo Yawk.

I looked at it and decided it was almost the same thing as the diced onion and tomato salad with vinegar and oil I was served for so many years when I was a jug-eared kid.

Breaking a Vow
over Tasty Melons

One of the solemn promises I made when I was a young'un is in grave danger. I said to myself: "Self, don't ever do like the old folks and prattle on about the good ole days and how cheap things used to be."

I was doing pretty good until this week, when I chanced upon a display of watermelons while shopping. My fingers tensed on the shopping cart . . . beads of sweat popped out on my forehead . . . splut, erg, splut . . . I'M NOT GONNA PAY THREE DOLLARS FOR A WATERMELON, NOT WHEN I ONCE BOUGHT SOME BY THE SIDE OF THE ROAD IN CORSICANA, TEXAS, TEN FOR A DOLLAR AND EVEN BETTER USED TO BUST 'EM FOR FREE ON MY UNCLE DAVID'S FARM IN GEORGIA, DAGNAB IT AND DOGGONE IT TO HELL, splut . . . ergonomics skognnb frimofrats and $*()%–#$!

I don't know where you grew up, but watermelons were a big, juicy part of the life of a Southern kid. When my grandpa would come home with a watermelon in a washtub full of crushed ice bought straight from the ice plant, well, I was one happy little jug-eared kid.

A major part of a Cracker education was to learn to "thump" watermelons to see if they were ripe.

I too learned the sound of a ripe watermelon and I am proud of the fact that I never have picked one that wasn't ripe, though I confess a couple of times I selected melons that were on the edge of overripe.

If buying from the Jacksonville farmer's market out under the viaduct on Beaver Street or from a roadside vendor, we would occa-

145

sionally confirm our judgment by pulling out a Barlow knife to cut a square plug in the melon and steal a taste.

Today, most vendors would not be thrilled at that custom.

There was also a lot of bargaining going on back then. If the farmer had a hand-lettered cardboard sign advertising four for a dollar, he knew that sharpsters like my folks were going to insist on five or even six for a dollar.

The abundance of Citrullus lanatus (yeah, I'm just showin' off with something I looked up in the encyclopedia) was such that watermelon cuttin's were a big part of every summer social calendar.

If you get a large group of kids around a large number of watermelons, you end up with a seed spittin' contest. I never quite got the hang of that and never was one of the top contenders. My cousins could shoot a seed all the way to the cemetery fence across the red clay road from the Memorial Free Will Baptist Church.

Seed spitting soon deteriorated into a watermelon fight, with screaming little hellions throwing watermelon rinds and sloppy gobs of red watermelon meat and seeds at each other.

The juice would soon turn clammy and sticky and on top of that, all the grown-ups would be giving stern lectures because the kids had turned into such damfools and messed up their Sunday clothes.

Enough daydreaming. I guess I should close this Sunday's offering by giving you a useful household hint to help soothe your grief at paying so much money for watermelons.

Pickles. Yep, my Aunt Dovie used to make the most wonderful watermelon rind pickles in Dixie. I still can see the Mason jars full of pickled watermelon rind sitting on the shelf with the sunlight shining through, giving the pickles a translucent glow.

And they were flavored with a wonderful combination of cinnamon, clove and allspice. Heck, if you have to pay that much for a watermelon, why throw anything useful away?

P.S. — Sorry about the tantrum. Actually, it may have opened up a whole new lifestyle for me. I think I'm gonna make one heck of a semi-crazed, ole coot someday (soon). I'm working on it.

Pan-frying Enterprises Beget Victuals Sublime

Health nuts may want to bail out now while there is still time. Food faddists and nervous nellies are given fair warning to flip to the Comics Section before it's too late. I'm a-fixin' to write about the importance of the frying pan in the kitchen of a Florida Cracker household.

If the mere mention of such greasy fare clogs your arteries or puffs out your waistline, it's already too late. I'm going to talk about good things to eat no matter how bad they are for you.

Who needs a pressure cooker, toaster oven or a crock pot?

Stove-top, pan-fried cornbread, fried chicken with milk gravy, battered and fried sliced green tomatoes, grilled cheese sandwiches fried in bubbling yellowish-brown butter, mashed potato pancakes and such were a big part of my Florida Cracker childhood. Notice that I left out the one which would offend you most: Hard-fried salt pork.

Apologists for this sort of cuisine may want to describe the method as "saute" but I say "saute, shmaute" because all it was, was fryin'.

The main use for the oven in the Carter family was for baking biscuits and sweet potatoes. Most everything else was done on top of the stove. And if it wasn't fried, there had to be a dern good reason. The only reason my folks didn't fry the turnip greens was because they wanted the pot likker.

Pot likker its own self is nothing to sneeze at. The water you fixed the greens in was often used to pour over a piece of pan fried cornbread. At my house, some chopped-up hot peppers, the nasty ones my grandpa grew next to the back doorstep, were thrown in, though I always preferred some hot pepper sauce.

None of this . . . fried food, pot likker, hellish peppers and all, is a recommended diet for anyone with a jumpy tummy.

Vegetables did not escape the pan-fry technique, either. I was raised on fried kernel corn, okra (dipped in cornmeal), squash and potatoes. Even something which previously had been baked did not escape. My folks liked to slice up baked sweet potato and pan-fry it until it was covered with "candy" made from its own syrup.

This was very popular, so much so that you could get a fork in the back of your hand sometimes while reaching for the last one.

Speaking of syrup and candy, my granddaddy always used that as an example of how poor he was growing up on a Georgia farm early in this century. He said he was so poor that he never ate a store-bought piece of candy until he was grown.

When he was a kid, his momma would pour some syrup into a hot frying pan on top of the old wood stove. The syrup would quickly caramelize and harden into a crude form of candy.

My Georgia kin stuck by the ole wood stove for many years after electrification, based on the theory that food cooked on one just tasted better. I can't argue with them, because the vittles were mighty tasty up at Uncle David and Aunt Dovie's farm.

Just some of the wonderful things that can come right off the top of a Cracker kitchen stove.

Eat Your Way to Good Luck in the New Year

I know how much y'all love it when I speak Latin and get all scientifical-like so . . .

Vigna senensis.

There! I said it and I'm glad.

"Self," you may be asking yourself, "What in the ever-lovin' heck is he writing about today." What it is, is nothing more or less than your chances for good luck for the rest of the year, that's all.

If you ignore this and go through the year with nothing but bad vibes, it's because you didn't have your Vigna senensis today.

That is the high falutin' name for one of my favorite dishes, the noble black-eyed pea.

No New Year was ever ushered into a Carter household without a steaming bowl of black-eyes, served with a generous helping of hog jowl or other side meat, or with rice in a traditional dish known as "Hoppin' John."

It was a custom in some Cracker homes to throw a dime in the "Hoppin' John," and the one that found it got extry-good luck in the coming year.

Heck, when I was a little jug-eared kid, I thought black-eyed peas came from the Piggly-Wiggly.

I don't know how they know it, but historians have an exact year, 1674, when black-eyes were introduced to the New World.

The City Island Library has a book of folklore and recipes called

149

"Kwanzaa: An African-American Celebration of Custom and Cooking." This tome has a neat section on "Hoppin' John," and author Eric Copage, despite working for the uppity Noo Yawk Times, has some info which rings true.

"South of the Mason-Dixon Line," Copage writes, *"the sign of a truly fine cook is whether he or she takes the hard way and cooks the rice directly in the beans or 'cheats' and cooks the rice separately."*

Copage says "Hoppin' John" is *"the most famous and myth-shrouded of African-American meals."*

Sheila Ferguson wrote a book on soul food that claims there was a man named John who would come hoppin' when his wife took the peas and rice off the stove. Another theory was that it was the young'uns who did all the hoppin' because it was suppertime and another theory that John was a waiter who performed various antics while serving.

In "Beans and Rice," author John Thorne quotes etymologists (Whoa! Ain't we high-falutin' now?) who say the name is a corruption of the French phrase "pois a pigeon," the Gallic term for pigeon pea. That's another name for Vigna senensis besides black-eye or cowpea.

Writer Edna Lewis has another theory, the one I found the most charming. She says "Hoppin' John" originated in South Carolina: *"Supposedly, 'Hoppin' John' was a cripple who peddled beans in the streets of Charleston and so a local dish made of red beans and rice was named for him."*

The black-eyes were later substituted for the red beans.

As for the New Year's Day superstition, Ms. Lewis says it originated in Africa, where bean dishes were often prepared for feast days and frequently were offered to various gods.

Despite all this emphasis on the Southeast, the black-eye is nowhere more revered than in East Texas, where it is the mainstay of one-dish meals, side dishes, salads and appetizers.

Most noteworthy of the last-named comestible is "Texas Caviar." That's pickled black-eyed peas that have been stored in the refrigerator for three days. I don't know about you, but it takes a lot of gumption to eat anything that has been stored in MY fridge for three days, but I reckon there ain't anything what can spoil a pickled black-eye.

In previous columns, I have told you about one of my favorite annual events, the Black-Eyed Pea Festival hosted by the piney-woods town of Athens, Texas. The festival has three divisions. The basic competition honors the best bowl of peas with side meat, such as hog jowl, hamhocks or white bacon. The second is the "Hoppin' John" category.

It's the third division that attracts the most notice. This is one that allows Texans to allow their very fertile imaginations to run wild. Typical entries are such things as Reunion Pea Casserole, Good Luck Jambalaya, Black-eyed Pea Dip, Mexi-Pea Salad and such.

I went to a festival back in the late 1960s and the winning Division Three entry that year was the Pea-Tini. It was gin and vermouth, garnished by a black-eyed pea on a toothpick.

It's thinking like that that made America great. Happy New Year y'all.

Key to Happiness:
Aunt Millie's Mango Bread Recipe

My mom and Aunt Millie were visiting relatives a few years ago up in the Panhandle. On the table were some particularly scrumptious cookies — sorta like shortbread cookies with slivers of almonds in them.

They were similar to the windmill cookies you could buy back when I was a little jug-eared kid growing up in Jacksonville.

Anyway, everybody was raving over the doggoned cookies and asking who brought them and asking what was the recipe.

The proud creator of the cookies was Aunt Pauline, who basked in the glory, but turned strangely silent when the subject of the recipe was broached.

After a long, painful delay, Aunt Pauline allowed as how she would share with the family, but "You know I usually get seven dollars for that recipe."

A family legend was born, and we still proudly serve "Aunt Pauline's Seven Dollar Cookies" for holidays and other celebrations.

I'm about to give you something far more valuable than seven dollar cookies. We have an even more important tradition going on my Momma's side of the family.

It's Aunt Millie's Mango Bread.

Most of you probably didn't know there was anything much you could do with a mango other than eat it out of hand (It's best if you are outside or standing in a bathtub when handling this juicy treat) or chunk it at a squirrel.

The noble mango, by the way, came to us from Southeast Asia by way of South America. It is known botanically as a member of the cashew family under the name Mangifera indica.

The mango isn't well known to many Americans, but actually is one of the most important and widely cultivated products in tropical climes. The name comes from the Portuguese, who adapted it from a Tamil word for the fruit encountered during the colonization of India.

Ol' Buddha his own se'f was once given a mango grove so that he might relax in its splendid shade. On the practical side, the mango is chock full of good nutrition, like vitamins A, C and D.

I thought I was in heaven when I saw all the mango trees in Hawaii, but I was disappointed when a Maui resident told me the ones there are inedible. The ones which grow in my Momma's back yard down in Hollywood are the juicy, sweet yellow and red kind. I love 'em.

Lots of folks say they don't like mango, but then they never tried my Aunt Millie's mango bread. It'll change your mind.

I get two or three loaves of mango bread from my beloved Aunt Millie every Christmas. I usually guard it jealously, and pretty much gronk it all down my own se'f.

In a fit of largess, I presented the most valuable Yule gift I've ever given to two of my friends at Daytona Beach City Hall last week. I gave one of my precious loaves of mango bread to Shirley Stickney and Gloria Marseglia, because they seemed so interested in mango bread as a concept.

Well, poor Gloria never got a clean shot at it. She took her half home and carelessly left it within range of her husband Paul. He took one taste and it was Gronk-o-rama!

Gloria turned around and found Paul guiltily licking his fingers and the half-loaf of mango heaven was history.

If someone who loves you can treat you this bad, think what a stranger could do.

Shirley didn't fare a whole bunch better. She did manage to salvage one slice before her kinfolk descended like locusts of the hapless half-loaf.

So there were hang dog looks at City Hall as Shirley and Gloria told me their tales of woe and mango bread deprivation.

Sorry, but I'm not giving up any more of my mango bread supply to anyone. When mango bread is outlawed, only outlaws will have mango bread. You'll get my last crumb of mango bread when my cold, dead fingers are pried from around it.

But I gave Gloria and Shirley something better. It's the key to your own ever-loving supply of mango bread, and now I'm going to share it with the world.

A few years ago, this recipe might not have done y'all a lot of good, because mango was hard to find. But I see it stocked in all the major supermarkets these days.

Herewith is the valuable recipe, making your Sunday News-Journal the best bargain in town. Hope y'all enjoy it:

AUNT MILLIE'S MANGO BREAD

Sift together in a large bowl: 4 cups of flour, 4 cups of sugar, 5 tsps. of cinnamon, 4 tsps. of baking soda and 1 tsp. of salt.

In a separate bowl, mix 2 and 1/4 cups of oil, 2 tsps. of lemon juice, 2 tsps. of vanilla and 7 eggs.

Mix with the dry ingredients and then add: 4 cups of diced mango, 1 cup of chopped walnuts and a cup of coconut.

Fold in the above ingredients and bake at 350 degrees for 1 hour. Yields four to six loaves or 10 to 12 mini-loaves.

Hey!!! Is this a full-service column or what? Doggone it, too much ain't enough!

Names of Some Bread-like Foods Can Be a Bit Misleading

Have you ever noticed how often I write about food? I know I do, but I can't help myself.

A case in point is the success of my Aunt Millie's Mango Bread recipe which I printed a few columns ago.

That stuff ought to be labeled a dangerous drug. Some of you readers have stopped me and told about how you baked up a few loaves and then gronked them all down in a feeding frenzy, sometimes with both hands and crumbs a-flyin'.

The only negative call was from folks who were confused by how dense and heavy mango bread is. I should have done a better job of explaining it's a lot like banana nut bread, a sort of cake, and not exactly like a loaf of Merita or anything.

My latest mango bread disciple is Phil Prial of New Smyrna Beach, who baked up a batch and went hog wild over it.

Many of you have seen Phil and his minions at the New Smyrna, Daytona Beach and Flagler farmer's markets purveying his own intoxicating creation called "The Real McCoy: Irish Soda Bread."

I had a nice chat with Phil on Friday afternoon and he told me about how he retired eight years ago after a career as a New York fireman along with wife Helen, who retired from her career as wife and mother to a family of eight.

Retirement drove Phil and Helen crazy. They couldn't sit still.

Helen enrolled in a nursing school and went on the teach nurse's aide courses.

Phil commandeered the kitchen at his local VFW hall and started baking Irish Soda Bread.

He got the recipe from his own sainted mother, who was born on the Emerald Isle.

This is not a small cottage industry. Phil and Helen produce about 150 loaves of soda bread a week. And they bake up even more when they go to festivals across the Southeast.

This may not strike you as a retirement, but Phil and Helen thrive on all the hard work. In fact, Phil laughs and jokes about the work and is grateful for it, though you can't always tell when he's teasing you because he is blessed with a bit o' the Irish blarney.

The upshot of all this is that Irish Soda Bread is misnamed too. It's heavy and goes real good with tea, its main purpose, and with coffee.

And a loaf of it is just as heavy as mango bread.

Another misnamed commodity, except in the other direction, is the hoecake, which is actually bread and not cake.

I got a wonderful letter from a friend in Ormond Beach and it included an excellent recipe and commentary on hoecake.

I tried to make hoecake at home. I set off the #@#$&#! smoke alarm twice and the hoecakes were black on one side and white on the other.

I yearn for the even brown texture the folks over at Hall's Lodge at the Astor Bridge can put on a hoecake.

Via a vintage cookbook entry from Appalachia, I'm told that boiling water is the secret to making great hoecake batter.

Four cups cornmeal, 1 tbs. bacon drippings, 1 tsp. salt and boiling water are the makin's, according to Sidney Farr of Stoney Fork, Kentucky, author of this recipe.

"Preheat oven to 425 degrees, scald cornmeal with enough boiling water to make a stiff dough, add bacon dripping and salt, stirring well. Shape into oval pones, one handful at a time and put in greased pan. Mother and Granny always left the imprints of their fingers across the tops. Bake until brown. The hoecakes may also be baked in a skillet on top of the stove, turning each pone to brown both sides."

I'll let y'all know how it comes out, but first I'm gonna remove the battery from that smoke detector.

Florida Faces
Sweet Potato Gap

Sometimes things don't turn out exactly the way you want them to.

Encouraged by some of you regular Sunday Punch buckaroos to stay on my investigation of the noble sweet potato, I worked my head to the bone only to come up with this disappointing fact.

Florida is not exactly your sweet potato capital of the cosmos, you understand. I checked with my friends at the Florida Institute of Food and Agricultural Sciences and received the sad news.

Sweet potatoes are not an important crop in the Sunshine State. A small crop is harvested in Dade County, but it is of the boniata variety used in Latin American cooking.

The annual sweet potato yield is such a small blip in the state's statistical bank, that an exact figure is not even listed.

Gall and bitter wormwoods. Drat!

Other states have us beat in that category. A North Central Mississippi hamlet of about 950 souls named Vardaman claims to be a Tater capital and has an annual festival saying so. I'll check that out as fodder for a future column.

North Carolina has such an affection for them that a bipartisan group of state reps banded together last year to make the sweet potato the official state vegetable.

The Tar Heel reps did not succeed in their Tater tribute, but I know their hearts were in the right place.

The most amazing hotbed of Tater consciousness is the San Joaquin

157

Valley of California. That's not a misprint. The Sweet Potato Council of California boasts that its farmers produce 12 percent of the nation's total harvest of the tasty tubers.

The University of California at Davis also devised one of the most unusual recipes I have ever seen for sweet potatoes. It's called a "Sweet Potato Burrito" (I'm not making this up, folks), and it has refried black beans, Monterey jack cheese and hot peppers as a complement to the diced yam.

Other recipes suggested by California growers are sweet potato salad, garlic mashed sweet potatoes, sweet potato and leek soup and sweet potato harvest pie.

I think I'll pass on most of those, but you can hand me a slice of that pie, thank you.

A few years back, I ran a recipe for sweet potato muffins I got from Joy Bergman back during one of my trips to the Pioneer Settlement for the Creative Arts over in greater downtown Barberville.

Response to that recipe was terrific, and it even spawned a variation authored by my favorite jurist, Circuit Court Judge McFerrin Smith. He folded in some whipped topping with the other ingredients and made a right smart sheet cake.

I have made Joy Bergman's sweet potato muffins my own se'f and I can tell you they are scrumptious. And I even made then wrong, putting in too much sugar and they came out great.

I guess that's the test of a great recipe, in that you can't goof it up no matter how hard you try.

Here's how: Combine 1 3/4 cups of self-rising flour, 1/2 cup of sugar, a tbsp. of brown sugar and 1/2 cup of chopped pecans in a large bowl and stir well. Then add 1 1/4 cup of cooked and mashed sweet potatoes, 3/4 cup milk, 1/4 cup melted butter and 2 eggs, beaten. Mix that up real good.

Spoon this batter into muffin pans, filling two-thirds full. Mix 1/4 cup of sugar and 1/2 tsp. of cinnamon and sprinkle some of that over each muffin. Bake at 425 degrees for 20 to 25 minutes.

And this is provided to you at no extra cost with your Sunday paper. Is this a full-service column or what? Too much ain't enough!

Recipe Stirs Many Jug-eared Tater Memories

Sweet potatoes were an important part of my jug-eared childhood, what with my Unca David being the sweet potato king of South Georgia and my grandpa insisting on baked taters being available in our Jacksonville Cracker kitchen day or night.

At night, I would occasionally walk into the kitchen and see ole H.D. Carter sitting there in his "long-hannelt underwear" peeling a sweet potato and dipping a cold biscuit into ribbon cane syrup or orange blossom honey.

A salad bowl filled with hot coffee sat on the side. He long ago had quit cups and saucers because it was too much trouble to get your coffee "saucered and blowed" the regular country way.

H.D. liked his sweet potatoes straight, no frills, no additives, sorta like the way he liked his whiskey and his friends. In the Carter kitchen, 90 percent of all taters were simply baked in their jackets, and peeled at the table or for midnight snacks.

My grandma and I would put a pat of butter on ours sometimes, but H.D. considered adding anything to a sweet tater a sacrilege. He never did. He would eat candied yams, but he wasn't really a big fan of those either. And he didn't care much at all for my grandmother's sweet potato souffle with tiny melted mushmellers on top, even though the rest of the family raved about it.

I have noticed that most of my Sunday readers aren't purists like ole H.D. Everybody has been raving about Joy Bergman's sweet potato

159

muffin recipe which I've conveyed in this column.

So I knew y'all would be all excitable if I shared the most recent message from Joy Bergman, who, as many of you know, is one of the nice folks who make the Pioneer Settlement over in Barberville such a wonderful place.

This week's tater delight is Sweet Potato Waffles with Orange Butter, and I'm going to tell you how to make them forthwith.

Here's the deal: Take 2 cups of all-purpose flour, a tbsp. of baking powder, 1/2 tsp. of salt and a dash of cream of tartar. Combine in a large bowl and set aside. Combine 3 egg yolks, 1 1/2 cups of cooked mashed sweet potatoes, a cup of milk, 1/4 cup of brown sugar and 1/4 cup of melted butter and stir into the flour mixture.

Beat 3 egg whites at room temperature until stiff peaks form and carefully fold into batter. Spread this batter on a pre-heated oiled waffle iron and cook until a light golden brown. This recipe should make about 8 waffles.

This recipe, which Joy says was originally sent to Southern Living magazine by a Houston, Texas tater gourmet, tastes best when accompanied by butter mixed with orange rind and honey.

I mentioned this interesting way of using sweet taters to his honor the judge at the courthouse the other day and the honorable McFerrin Smith spoke right up with what sounds like a neat idea.

"That sounds like it would be good if you sprinkled a few pecan pieces on top," the judge ruled. I agreed, and suggested maybe even a dollop of whipped cream.

All this talk of pecans, whipped cream and orange butter wouldn't have done much for the jaded taste buds of the late H.D. Carter, I reckon, but that's okay. All of you regular Sunday Punch buckaroos are much more creative in your search for ways to enjoy the noble yam what am.

Yam Search Heads out of World

Yams From Outer Space.

You've read in this column about how sweet potatoes are out of this world, but this is ridiculous.

Yams From Outer Space is actually a Blacksburg, Virginia, alternative rock band I found while cruising the Internet for sweet potato lore.

This is an, errr . . . ummm, eclectic group. "Yams" has produced albums with names like "Rug Fibre" and "Domesticating Your Rhino."

Inspired by the great spirit of Frank Zappa, this team of tunesmiths does mostly original stuff, but has been known to break into a soulful rendition of "Rubber Duckie" of Muppet fame, or Madonna's "Like A Virgin."

There is no sensible explanation about how the band got its name.

Thank goodness for places like Media, Pennsylvania, just up the road from Blacksburg and the home of the sane, sensible Sweet Potato Cafe. This redoubtable eatery is an oasis in the midst of a sea of strip malls.

Here is a review put on the Net by a Swarthmore College student, apparently. *"One of my favorite places in Media is the Sweet Potato Cafe, a place where you can get sweet potato as a side order to everything and they also have free ice water, no questions asked . . . If you go on Fridays around lunchtime there may be somebody up in the front singing with a guitar."*

Yeah, but can he do "Rubber Duckie" or "Like A Virgin?"

161

I surfed around for more 'tater facts. It was a veritable cornucopia. Want the fixins for the famed sweet potato pie at the Taylor House Inn in Wilmington, North Carolina?

It's there, along with a slew of other recipes. Most of the pie instructions contain vanilla extract as an ingredient. That reminded me of the scolding I got from The News-Journal librarian when I let slip the secret of her famous Mallory sweet potato pies in a recent column.

Apparently the substitution of lemon extract for vanilla makes the pies especially good, but nobody outside the family was supposed to know that.

So I'm correcting that column. Folks, forget what I said about lemon extract. I wasn't s'posed to write that.

Emotions run pretty high, sweet potato pie wise. You remember the big deal over at Daytona Beach City Hall when Emory Counts and Ronnie Sharpe started the "Pie Challenge."

Emory bought his at Morrison's and Ronnie brought in one baked by her mother, so I don't think this argument has been settled yet. Another pie challenge is in the works for this fall, I believe.

Well, forget about the Blacksburg Sound, strip mall cafes, The Taylor House and City Hall. Today's featured Sunday Punch heroine lives out Osteen way.

She wrote me a wonderful letter about a Salisbury, Maryland, institution called English's Restaurant. Since 1935, this fine cafe has consistently produced some of the finest Chicken 'N Dumplin's in Frank Perdue Country.

Every Thursday is proudly proclaimed "Chicken 'N Dumplin's Day."

Guess what comes with your entree? Why, it's sweet potato biscuits, of course.

Here's how to make up a larrupin' batch of about five dozen of these little lovelies:

Cook enough sweet potatoes to produce about 7 cups of mashed 'tater. Step 1 is to combine the mashed potato with 2 1/2 cups of sugar, 2 cups of margarine, and 3 1/2 tablespoons of baking powder.

Step 2 is to mix in at low speed 6 1/2 cups of all-purpose flour and 1/4 tablespoon of soda. Refrigerate one hour.

Step 3 is to roll the dough on a floured surface. Cut with a biscuit cutter or a plastic tumbler. Place on a greased baking pan and bake in a 350 degree oven for 15 to 18 minutes.

There you are. Another great food tip at no extra cost from your favorite Sunday newspaper.

Recalling a
Garden of Delights

A News-Journal buddy brought a box of persimmons to the office the other day and gave them away to sundry colleagues. You guessed it . . . the sight of those succulent, deep orange p'simmons sent me on another visit down ole memory lane.

Memory lane in this case actually is Marion Road up in the country of Duval, where my folks owned a great old beast of a house that was much too big for our small family, but we enjoyed it nevertheless.

The rumor was that the house had once been a speakeasy during Prohibition and that a nightclub thrived after hours in the basement for many years. There were a few ghost stories and rumors of gang-land-style violence associated with the place, which made it even more fun for me.

The house and the four acres surrounding it had something for everybody. We had a boathouse and dock on Big Pottsburg Creek where my granddaddy enjoyed boating and fishing. There was plenty of room for my grandmother's prize camellias and azaleas and I enjoyed it all.

The pecan trees furnished a major cash crop every two years, and one of the times I got to keep the money. There were tangerine, orange and grapefruit trees all over the place. One driveway took visitors under a grape arbor.

Little kumquat bushes appeared here and there and two very large persimmon trees stood just off the south side of the spacious front porch. At the other end of the porch was a veritable tree which went up above the roof and my grandmother boasted that it most likely was the largest and oldest japonica camellia bush in the world, though I later found out this also most likely was stretching the truth quite a bit.

Along the terraced hillside going down to the riverbank stood fig trees which were the focus of occasional battles between the Carters and the local blue jay and mockingbird population. The birds generally were the winners, although I usually rescued enough unpecked fruit to make several jars of preserves.

The figs were placed on a shelf next to the Mason jars of pears, apple butter, kumquat preserves, watermelon rind preserves and pepper jelly which my grandma had made or were contributed to the cause by our Georgia kin.

I had picked the pears myself up in Georgia from the two huge trees next to the field where my country cousins and I used to bust watermelons. They were hard, gritty little sand pears which weren't all that tasty for eatin' in hand.

But they made bodacious "preserves," as my Aunt Dovie said, and they were often part of our breakfast fare, to be slathered generously on a piece of hot buttered toast or wedged inside a fresh-baked biscuit.

It's hard to say which of these was my favorite. I consider the satsuma the highest form of citrus and we boasted three trees of those tangy treats. I loved to pick them fresh from the tree right after a frost and they were so cold it hurt your teeth.

But there's a special place in my heart, as there used to be on the kitchen windowsill, for the golden persimmons of my youth. The recent treasure trove reminded me once more of the long wait for the 'simmons to get ripe enough to eat.

I remember clearly the terrible "wrongstert outerds" feeling if you got puckered by a green 'un but the almost unbearable joy of getting all sloppy eating a good 'un. The waiting was a large part of the whole thing.

A watched persimmon ripens very slowly. That's still true even though this little jug-eared kid long ago was driven out of his Marion Road eden into the ordinary, work-a-day world of adults.

The more things change, the more they stay the same.

Resolution Prompts Study of Ice Cream

I'm only making one resolution this new year and, frankly, I don't believe I'll be able to keep it.

Here it is. I promise not to bring any butter pecan ice cream into the house for a whole year!

This resolution more or less was forced on me by Madame Queen, who has so little willpower, butter-pecan-wise, that her only defense is not to have it within three miles of the house.

This confection fixation led me to do some research. How many other Americans have a serious butter-pecan abuse problem? The answer was surprising. Not many.

According to statistics released by an ice cream trade group, here are the top 15 most popular flavors: Chocolate marshmallow, rocky road, coffee, chocolate almond, cherry, praline pecan, fudge ripple, cookies and cream, French vanilla, chocolate chip, Neapolitan, strawberry, butter pecan, chocolate and the No. 1 . . . vanilla!

Strawberry and butter pecan are tied at 5.3 percent, chocolate flirts with the 10 percent mark and vanilla is the clear winner at 29 percent. In fact, if one combines the vanilla and French vanilla category, that totals one-third of all the ice cream consumed.

I once created a theory I dubbed "Baskin-Robbins Syndrome" to describe the societal problems sometimes brought on by too many choices in our daily lives. Though we are surrounded with an amazing cafeteria of things to do and be, some folks (maybe, say, about one-

166

third of the population?) settle for just plain vanilla.

But is that such a bad thing? Not really, if one considers the more noble aspects of the vanilla bean. Though vanilla is often associated with the humdrum or plain aspects of life, it actually is one of the most dynamic flavors in nature.

I remember the old-fashioned ice cream churns at the Dinner on the Ground at Memorial Free Will Baptist Church in Surrency, Georgia. The adults would enlist us little jug-eared kids as cheap labor. We would turn the crank in exchange for the right to lick the dasher.

There is no longer wait in the world for a little kid than to wait for hand-churned ice cream to be ready for eating. We'd grab bowls of the stuff and eat it so fast we'd get the (Gasp!) dreaded "ice cream headache." But it was worth it.

Vanilla comes from an orchid grown in exotic places like Madagascar, Mauritius, the South Pacific and Central America. The Spanish conquistadors first discovered it in Mexico, where it was used as a form of tribute paid to Aztec royalty.

The first ice creams are believed to have been made from snow in China in 200 B.C. and a later version of fruit juice and snow is credited to the Roman Emperor Nero.

Marco Polo, it is said, first combined some of the Chinese water ices with milk. By the 1600s, ice cream was such a delicacy that King Charles I of England offered his cooks jobs for life if they made ice cream for him and then kept it a secret.

Our little trip down the caloric memory lane now moves to New York City in 1776, where attention was paid not only to the formation of a new nation, but the opening of the first ice cream parlor.

Maybe this explains why George Washington had false teeth: The Father of our Country was an ice cream addict who once ran up a $200 bill (in 1700s dollars) one summer.

Dolly Madison was quite the hit when she served up mounds of ice cream at the second inaugural ball in 1812. A lady named Nancy Johnson made sundries history in 1846, when she invented the hand-cranked freezer. She didn't have enough capital to market it herself, so she sold the patent for $200.

Five years later, Jacob Fussell opened the first commercial ice cream plant in Baltimore. In 1921, new immigrants arriving at Ellis Island were served ice cream as their first truly American meal.

It is truly American, and we are world leaders in this regard, consuming nearly 23 quarts capita per year. A man named Dennett D'Angelo is the pacesetter, setting the world record by gobbling three pounds, six ounces of ice cream in 90 seconds.

Wow! Now there is a dreaded "ice cream headache" to conjure with.

Bitter Fruit Sparks Many Sweet Times

One of the favorite tricks I used to play on other kids visiting from "up North" was to pick some kumquats off a tree and hand them out.

I would bite down on mine, but was very careful to eat only the peel, which was fairly sweet, and the only part I liked. My victims would assume that the kumquat was nothing more than a tiny orange or tangerine and would take a healthy bite down into the sour, lemony pulp.

It was a great trick to play on furriners, and I loved the puckery faces they made when surprised by their first encounter with Fortunella margarita, better known as the Negami Kumquat.

After I grew up, I began to appreciate other uses of the interesting little citrus fruit. Kumquat preserves go very well with your breakfast toast, and the fruit is used in chutneys, relishes, pies and a host of other ways.

My personal favorite is as a substitute for lemon in iced tea.

The small trees are very handsome and used as an ornamental shrub in many South Florida yards.

Many Floridians like to keep a small kumquat shrub in the back yard and use the fruit both for eating and for holiday decorations.

Any time I see a kumquat tree with fruit on it, and right now is prime time for the odd little trees, I pick one and eat the slightly sweet peel and throw the tart pulp away.

Kumquats tend to ripen between December 15 and April 15, and late January is really prime time, and (you guessed it) the basis of a festival.

Y'all already know how much I love "festibles," and there is one coming up in honor of the underappreciated kumquat on January 28-29.

You might think that such a citrusfest would occur down near Miami, or at least in the Indian River area famous for other types of citrus.

But you would be wrong. The self-proclaimed "kumquat capital of the world" is a little burg called St. Joseph, just 30 minutes north of Tampa, near Dade City in Pasco County.

I don't exactly see a host of towns lining up to contest that claim, so I'll go along with it. I guess it might be sort of like our "World's Most Famous Beach" tag. Who wants to take the trouble to fight us over it?

Growers in and around St. Joseph ship thousands of bushels of kumquats around the world, and for three years have hosted a festival to brag about it.

"It's sweet on the outside and tart on the inside," proclaims a press release from the Dade City Chamber of Commerce. *"It's being featured as a trendy new flavor and ingredient in some of the top magazines, including Gourmet and New Woman magazines. It's Florida's tiniest citrus product."*

At last year's gala, 20 cooks used kumquats in creative ways such as a seasoning for meat and veggies and as an ingredient in salads and desserts.

I hope this doesn't ruin your breakfast, but a couple of the recipes were for Kumquat and Rum Ice Cream and Kumquat and Maple Syrup Shortbread. There also were Kumquat Chips, Kumquat Pound Cake and Kumquat Salsa.

This little showcase of Floridiana is proving quite popular. More than 20,000 folks show up for the doggoned thing every year.

I think that proves my theory that everybody loves a festival, especially one with an offbeat premise. I know these events never fail to capture my attention.

Sunday Punch is a full-service column, as all of you veteran readers know, so I'll close with some amazing nutritional information.

Each kumquat contains about 12 calories, and I'm assuming most of those are in the peel, which is surprisingly pleasant. There are traces of carbohydrate, protein and fiber, but kumquats are power-packed when it comes to potassium, Vitamin A and Vitamin C.

And I'll close by answering the question y'all have been wondering about. what does the word "kumquat" mean? Well, the good folks who run the festival say it is a Chinese word which translates as "golden orange."

I guess that's a lot more romantic than "sour face," huh?

Love Affair with Peaches Doesn't Rot

Some cyber-friends and I were recently exchanging e-mail and some witty posts and ripostes were based on the lyrics to an old Steve Miller Band song, "The Joker."

One of the stanzas from that song, made famous by one of the great nonsense lines in rock music history, *"the pompitous of love,"* goes as follows:

"You're the cutest thing
That I ever did see
I really love your peaches
Want to shake your tree"

Those words always bring back memories of my late grandfather, H.D. Carter, the squire of Surrency, Georgia, whose favorite saying went along those lines. Anytime someone criticized H.D., or indicated ways that he could improve himself, he would reply: "If'n you don't like my peaches, you don't have to shake my tree."

That gibe was often aimed at my grandmother, a refined Southern matron who recoiled in horror at H.D.'s terrible grammar, lapses in profanity, his habit of dipping snuff and the pint of Seagram's 7 he kept in the glove compartment of his pickup truck.

Peaches were a big part of my childhood.

Our Georgia kin had peach trees in the yard, and they were not only a source of pleasure, but of pain. When any of us young'uns would misbehave, we were sternly ordered to go in the back yard and break off a peach switch and bring it in to be used on our little legs and back-sides.

We were warned that if the switch we fetched was not satisfactory, then Daddy or Granddaddy would go in the yard and get one that would strike terror in the hearts of all young miscreants.

The damned little knobs and knots on a peach branch raised welts that didn't go away for days.

But that was the only negative about this noble fruit tree. It still evokes warm memories of peach cobblers cooling on the windowsill and hand-churned peach ice cream or simply taking one straight from the tree, so juicy and sweet that you almost had to stand in the bathtub while eating it.

H.D. was proud of his Georgia roots. And he loved the nickname "Peach State."

He would triumphantly return from visits to the farm with bushel baskets full of peaches. We would eat as many as possible before they spoiled and the rest would be sliced and frozen for pies and cobblers later in the year.

If he were alive today, he would not be pleased to learn that Georgia is the "Peach State" in name only, and that his beloved birthplace is third in peach production. South Carolina is second and, most bitter of wormwoods, California is first.

And a historical note I found this week would vex him mightily. Peaches were introduced to the New World, not in Georgia, but in Florida. Yep, ole Chris Columbus his own se'f had some delivered to St. Augustine during his second and third voyages.

I don't know if I've just been lucky or what, but it's my opinion that the peaches we've been getting this summer are the best I've tasted in many years.

I bought some from roadside stand, the supermarket and stole a few that a friend brought here in the newsroom a while back. They were magnificent.

As most of you regular Sunday Punchers know, I am a great admirer of Thomas Jefferson, chief among all of our founding fathers. It's a little-known fact that Jefferson was an admirer of the peach and once nominated it for a high honor. Well, read for yourself:

In his diary entry of 12 July 1781, Thomas Jefferson wrote: *"I am now convinced that our great nation must have a National Fruit. Mr. Adams recommends the apple, for it is noble. Mr. Hancock recommends the pear, for it is plentiful. Mr. Franklin recommends the passionfruit, but he would. No, I cannot waver from my conviction that the Peach shall reign supreme above all."*

Okraphobes Give Bad Rap to Tasty Pods

A couple of weekends ago, I harvested a few okra pods from my Unca Jimmy's garden down at Lake Okeydokey, and it brought back memories of the raison d'etre (I know y'all really love it when I speak French, and I'll have more later) of the first Sunday Punch column back in 1984.

I took to the typewriter then to make a stirfry defense of the noble Hibiscus esculentus (you get really turned on when I speak Latin too, I bet) from a dastardly sneak attack by a dark cabal of okraphobes. It was shortly after my reasoned and reasonable defense of the venerable veggie that the podbusters replied by filling my desk with several pounds of rotting okra salvaged from a farmer's market trash pile.

I add that note only to give you a hint of the depths to which okra-phobes will go to take cheap podshots at the object of their obsession. But I continue to take the high ground in this ongoing debate and will not stoop to negative campaigning.

To keep things on a high plane, I have gathered a bushel of factoids from such wide-ranging and reliable sources as encyclopedias and cookbooks to make my case. As many of you already know, much of the okra-bashing results from the negative feelings (some down-right Fruedian) that folks have about the so-called "slime" inside the okra pod.

Well, slime is as slime does, but I prefer to refer to this substance by its correct technical term in civilized debate, to wit, mucilage.

My okreducation was recently expanded by reading a book authored by Chef Bert Greene, who devotes an entire chapter to okra. He reports the veggie came to the New World from Africa.

Ancient Arab physicians believed that okra seeds had therapeutic properties which, once consumed, floated through the body forever. Okra was deemed a delicacy that was prepared only for special occasions such as weddings and baptisms. The Arab name for okra, uehka, means "a gift."

The pods were so highly prized in what is today known as Angola that wars were fought over them.

The first formal okra recipe was made by Abul-Abbas el Nebati his own se'f, a Spanish Moor from Seville (the one in Spain, not the one in Northwest Volusia County) in the 13th century. This notable recipe was called "basiyah" and was a stew composed mainly of okra and apricots.

Today, the noble pods are considered low-rent staples of Cajun and cracker cookery, but I hasten to point out a more sophisticated and urbane cuisine.

(Here comes the French again, just like I promised . . .)

Okra is featured prominently in "The World Authority," or the mother of all cookbooks, the Larousse Gastronomique. In its pages are such taste tempters as "Gombos Braises Au Gras." That's okra braised with bacon, y'all. Larousse features other savories such as okra with cream, in butter, "a la creole" and "a la tomate."

And there is my personal favorite, "Gombos Aux Fritots." That's fried okra, son, and it's tres bien . . . magnifique as all get out.

According to my calculations, the world is perfectly split on the subject of okra. Not counting me, half of all living souls today love okra and the other half detest it. The number of undecided is zero, and there is not one who merely likes or dislikes okra.

So, with a double blast from the Sunday Punch bassoon (Blatttt! Phoooot!), I hereby cast the tie-breaking vote in favor of okra. We gumbo-lovers are now the majority party and will brook no more nonsense from the minority podbusters.

The Knights of the Hibiscus no longer will allow cheap podshots to go unanswered. The feeling is mucilage.

Warm Childhood Memories Stirred by Toast Sensation

Why am I thinking so much about food lately? Grits, hush puppies and sugar cane have dominated the last few Sunday Punch columns, and when I was working my head to the bone thinking about this week's humble offering, I kept thinking about toast.

Not the kind you make with champagne, but plain old toast. Broiled bread. Old-time radio fans may remember the droll comedy team of Bob & Ray. One of their funniest bits was about a turnpike restaurant called "The International House of Toast." The specialite' de la maison (I know how much y'all love it when I speak French) was Toast-on-a-Stick.

I don't know why it was never marketed. I think it's a sure fire winner.

Toast is one of those warm and fuzzy memories of childhood. It speaks of early mornings in the kitchen, with the comforting smell of bread in the toaster and coffee perking and birds starting to tweet outside the window.

There is mother's love in toast. Someone once wrote a book titled "Mommies Love Burnt Toast" because Mom was always the first to volunteer to scrape the burnt pieces for herself and leave the prime, golden brown slices for the rest of the family.

We had one of those old-fashioned two-slice pop-up toasters when I was a kid. I didn't like it. The toast came out too dry and sometimes a piece of bread would get caught, jamming the mechanism and forc-

177

ing you to risk electrocution by jamming a case knife into the slot to extricate the by-then charcoal black remains.

I was a big fan of oven toast, buttered ahead of time so it would sink into the bread. Butter-yellow in the center and dark brown on the edges, it was the bestest kind.

Sometimes I would eat the crisp edge first, leaving a butter-soaked soft center for one last calorie-loaded gulp. Toast that good could be eaten right out of the oven with nothing added, but the Carter table always boasted some great toasty companions.

Like fig preserves we made fresh from the trees in our back yard. And my grandma's favorite guava jelly, and preserves we made out of those gritty ole sand pears picked at my uncle's Georgia farm. Sometimes we had fresh apple butter and orange blossom honey.

Sometimes there were special treats, like cheese toast. Cholesterol haters should turn away now, because sometimes we got cheese melted on buttered toast, or on toast slathered with mayonnaise. I don't care what anybody says. It was good.

My momma's little variation was a treat she called "Cheese Dreams" and it's true I still dream about them today. On special days, my brother Danny and I would come to a kitchen table where Mom would have a tray of toast, each topped with cheddar cheese, a red-ripe tomato slice and two pieces of bacon making a big X in the middle.

Well, as you might imagine, we were two happy little jug-eared kids.

If we had company, my grandparents would lay out a big Sunday feed. Right in the middle of the table was a huge tray of toast. In addition to all the goodies I mentioned earlier, my grandma would fix a big bowl of sausage gravy, or creamed chipped beef (I loved SOS even when I was in the Air Force) and sometimes chicken a la king.

Sometimes my plate would be covered with toast, in some stage of preparation; one plain buttered, one with fig preserves on it, one with cheese on it and another smothered in sausage gravy. It was Toast-a-rama!

I saved the best for last. My all-time favorite toastiferous memory is spiked with, ahhh, cinnamon. I think cinnamon toast must indeed be the food of the gods.

In ancient times, cinnamon was more valuable than gold. I think I know why.

My kids inherited my love for cinnamon toast, and that is the basis of one of our family's pet stories. At about the same time they were old enough to clamor for the treat, David, Karen and Ginger spent a lot of time teasing each other about monkeys.

When they would see photos or cartoons of monkeys they would squeal with delight and get into "am not" and "you are, too" arguments about who displayed the most primate traits.

About that time, Ginger came up with her little trick of calling her favorite breakfast treat "simian toast." When we would go out to restaurants, that's what she would order, and as the waitress walked away, Ginger would put her little hands up to her mouth and giggle: "I said simian toast and she didn't even notice."

There would be another round of giggling and finger pointing when the waitress would return with the hot, pungent toast. Then all the giggling ceased and greedy little hands reached out to capture all the simian toast pudgy little fingers could handle.

Life was good. Good enough to, say, propose a toast.

The Paralysis that Choice Hath Wrought

I went to this really neat restaurant and I liked the food a lot, but there was one hassle. Ordering was a real chore. All I wanted was a simple ham and cheese sandwich, but I soon found out nothing was simple.

"Do you want the sandwich on white, wheat or rye bread?" asked the bright, freckle-faced waitress.

My reply: "Umm. Rye bread."

"Jewish, Westphalian or regular?"

"Hmmm. Just plain ole rye bread, I guess."

"Mustard, mayonnaise or horseradish sauce?"

"Well, mustard would be nice."

"Yellow, brown or cajun spice?"

"Brown."

"Swiss, cheddar or blue cheese?"

"Swiss."

"Finnish, Jarlsberg or New York?"

"Jarlsberg."

"Lettuce, tomato or onion?"

I'm starting to weaken. My voice rises at the end so I'm saying "Lettuce?" with a question mark, even though I'm supposed to be furnishing a decisive answer.

The waitress is unfazed. Her smile never wavers. "Bibb, iceberg or endive?" she coos.

180

My mind races . . . which one is the plain type of lettuce you usually buy in supermarkets. I think it's iceberg, so I tentatively say: "Iceberg?"

"Pickles, olives or peppers?"

"Uhhh. Olives?"

"Green, black or Greek?"

"Green, I think . . . Ma'am, can I ask you to do me a big favor?"

"Sure, what is it?"

"Would you please just bring me a ham and cheese sandwich. I don't care what it has on it as long as it generally fits the description of a ham and cheese sandwich. Any kind of ham. Any kind of cheese. Any kind of bread."

She looked at me funny, like I was crazy or something. And I guess I was. Like most Americans I become either frozen with indecision or filled with indignation when offered too many choices.

A couple of friends who were with me that night say that because of the beer we had with the sandwiches, my memory may have added a few embellishments to the story above and it's not strictly true. Maybe they are right. But that's sorta the way I remember it.

I am sure most of you have fallen victim to forms of the malady, which I have named "Baskin-Robins Syndrome." By that I mean most people would be really hacked if the only ice cream flavor available was vanilla, yet many people order vanilla at shops like Baskin-Robbins, of all places.

Thirty-two flavors with cutesy names like "Berry Berry Good To Me" and "Egg Drop Delite" and every taste sensation from toffee coffee amaretto swirl to barbecue bean is laid out in front of you and the paralysis sets in. Many look nervously at the floor and cough, then order two scoops of vanilla.

Have you ever checked out the vacant stares in the cereal section of the supermarket. From Frankenberry to Granola Trail Mix, the multitude of choices is staggering. Sometimes, the haggard customer slowly reaches out for a familiar box of corn flakes or popped rice and shuffles off.

Indecision is a terrible thing.

Back when there was only one football, baseball or basketball game on television each week, I was an avid viewer. I planned my schedule around the games, and it didn't matter who was playing.

Today, I am sometimes faced with the choice of five or six games on some evenings or weekends, and end up skipping them all. The choice is even more intimidating when I visit my Uncle Frank and Aunt Claudean down at the lake, 'cause they own a satellite dish. Social scientists are telling us that the paralysis brought on by too many choices may be a threat to our freedoms. They warned that infinite choice leads to passivity and conformity rather than dynamic diversity. Angered and weary of having to make too many decisions from too many lists with too many items, Americans may long for the comforts of having those decisions made for them.

Maybe that's why so many of us who love freedom are trying to simplify our lives in an age of overwhelming complexity. Maybe Kris Kristofferson was right *"Freedom's just another name for nothin' left to lose, and nothin' ain't worth nothin' but it's free."*

Tasting the Flavors of Youth: Moon Pie and Watermelon

Back in the 1940s, my grandfather would take me on weekend trips back to his Georgia birthplace, Appling County.

I was always impressed when he went down a red clay road just south of Surrency and he would point out a derelict old house, which by then was mostly a pile of gray, weathered boards.

H.D. Carter would spit tobacco juice into the weeds choking a collapsed wooden fence in the front yard and drawl: "That's the house where I was borned in 1897."

We'd get back into the car and drive down the washboard road until we hit a narrow bridge without any railings and some of the boards were rotted or broken and they would rattle real loud and I would hold my breath every time until we got over it.

H.D. considered it a noble, sturdy bridge and never hesitated to drive over it any time he wanted. I was again impressed.

If it was the right time of years, we'd stop at one of my Uncle David's fields and bust some watermelons. We'd eat the hearts out of them and leave the parts with all the seeds alone.

It was wasteful, but there were lots of watermelons and they were cheap then.

Along one side of the watermelon patch was a couple of sand pear trees. I'd fill up a sack with sand pears, which were gritty and not all that good to eat out of hand, but my grandma could make some really great preserves out of them.

183

We always had homemade pear and fig preserves on the table when I was growing up. I feel sorry for anybody who didn't.

When we would hit an intersection with the dusty, red clay road that would eventually take you to Baxley, the county seat, there was a wondrous sight.

Right out there in the middle of nowhere, and you wondered how in the world anyone could ever make a living, there was Miss Birdie's gas station.

Visiting Miss Birdie was always a treat any my grandfather liked to stop to talk with the spitters and whittlers who solved all the problems of the world there.

H.D. told me once that she was "a widder woman," which I later figured out meant that her husband had died and left her a store.

When we went to see Miss Birdie, I always begged H.D. to buy some gas and let me pump it. Miss Birdie's station still had one of those old-fashioned gas pumps, where you filled a big glass bowl at the top to a certain level and then let gravity feed it into your car's tank.

The neat gas pump and the ice cold Co-Colas and the big Moon Pies were reason enough to go to Miss Birdies, but my larcenous heart had another target in mind.

Miss Birdie had a punchboard.

Long before Lotto and World Series pools, punchboards were the weakness of many country gamblers. It was a thick piece of cardboard with little compartments in it. They were illegal, which made me want to play them even more.

They came with something like a Spam key, which you used to punch out one of the little honeycombed compartments.

Inside was a rolled-up little piece of paper about the size of a fortune in a Chinese cookie. It told you if you had won a prize.

H.D. and I would then head home, with a car all gassed up, a bag of sand pears in the back seat, a couple of punchboard papers (losers!) on the floorboard and my stomach full of watermelon, Moon Pie and Co-Cola.

Life was good for a little jug-eared kid and his grandpa back in the 1940s.

The Pink Brigade

Flamingo

The downy pink cloud
Balanced on a toothpick
Encircled by cool blue water wreaths
Under a fan of emerald palm
Transforms into a pink
grapefruit sunburst
Spreading watermelon wings
Brilliant as the sunrise
The rare pink pearl of the tropics
Greets the new citrus sun.

Melanie Moore's free verse, titled, very succinctly and I think tastefully, "Flamingo"

— JC

It's Time to Take a Stand Against Yard Flamingo Bias

An outrage! A base canard! A heinous act not in harmony with the geometry and theology of the Universe!

Right here in River City, folks, your Friday morning Journal ran a front page headline indicating that yard flamingos are tacky. It was fitting that such a nifty color photo of our only native Florida art form be on the front page, but then an editor who may be beyond hope of rehabilitation labeled it "Vogue Tackiness."

I object. And I know that all right thinking native Floridians join me in this protest.

A society which does not prize lawn statuary is doomed. At their heights, Greece and Rome excelled in the production of lawn ornamentation. But have you noticed that most of the garden statues in those countries are weathered, broken or in disrepair?

And they aren't world powers any more, either.

Coincidence, or what?

This column long has been a bastion (In fact, a reader called me a bastion just last week!) of pro-flamingo sentiment. Think pink. Pinkpeace. 'Mingo Power. Yay for the Yardbirds.

And there are readers out there who have faithfully written to share their love for the yard flamingo, cement or plastic.

Anybody who lays a finger on a single feather of our state yardbird is on the fightin' side of me. If it were left to me to choose a government without flamingos or flamingos without government, I would

187

unhesitatingly choose the latter.

Love me, love my 'mingos. I used to feel sorry for myself because I had no class, but then I met a man who had no flamingos.

I'm pink, therefore I am. When flamingos are outlawed, only outlaws will have flamingos.

Yard flamingos on Flagler Beach.

Flaming Flamingos! Papa's Proud of Pink Progeny

A longtime dream has been realized. Fulfillment is mine after all these years.

I feel like passing out cigars or somesuch.

I'm the proud papa of a pair of pink progeny. For the first time in my life I own two yard flamingos — prime examples of Florida's only native art form. I am quietly proud.

Their names? How good of you to ask. My yard guardians have been dubbed Stan and Ollie.

My former domicile — a condo in Ormond Beach — was in a narrow-minded neighborhood. The folks there, banded in a very hostile brace of homeowners' associations, were veritably prejudiced against yard statuary in all forms. Pity.

But now that I have made good an escape from the clutches of those two expensive homeowners' groups — it was sort of a double clutch on the wallet every three months, and then there was that nasty $600 special assessment just before Christmas one year — I am re-establishing a distinguished tradition.

Now that I'm firmly ensconced on terra firma owned only by me and my friendly mortgage company, I am sponsoring the rebirth of "Melody Ranch."

The old Melody Ranch never had yard flamingos, and that's a deficiency I took care of this week. Those cute little boogers have a prime viewing spot in the yard.

189

I can't wait until I am totally moved into the new digs. I'm gonna grab my Sunday paper (The News-Journal, of course. How tacky of you to even think any different!) and a cup of coffee, then throw a Willie Nelson record on the turntable and stretch out in an easy chair on the porch.

It'll be mighty satisfying and restful to wile away the early morning hours watching Stan and Ollie graze among the ferns. It don't get no better'n this.

Stan and Ollie at home.

When in Rome, Sport Fabulous Fuchsia Flamingo Fashions

The leadership position of this humble column in behalf of Florida's only native art form — the yard flamingo — is assured. Word has spread as far away as Rome.

OK, OK. So it's Rome, GEORGIA, we're talking about, but that still doesn't diminish my joy at the good publicity this column has provided for our fabulous fuchsia friends.

An enterprising clothing wholesaler from that Georgia city was in Daytona Beach this week looking for retail outlets for his line of sportswear. The distinctive part of this clothing line is the tastefully embroidered brace of flamingos placed where Izod does its alligator and Ralph Lauren puts his polo pony.

"I heard you write a lot about flamingos," said David Callaway as he brought his samples into the newsroom. "That's right," I growled in my best reportorial style. "Carter's the name and flamingos are my game."

Turns out young David (he's 28) got his start in the design, screening and embroidery biz while working his way through Auburn University. I was happy to hear that because an occasional cry of "War Eagle" is nowhere near as irritating as the incessant cries of "How 'bout them DAWGS" normally emanating from the Greater Rome Area.

An astute observer of what's hot and what's not, David decided the time was ripe for a line of polo shirts and such featuring our pink feathered friends. He made a few sales to Atlanta stores last week and late this week was still knocking on doors here and in St. Augustine and Ponte Vedra Beach.

Upcoming sales junkets are planned for Fort Lauderdale, Palm Beach and other South Florida fashion hotspots. He also will be working closely with some campus stores and sporting goods shops.

David's business card lists him as vice president of Special Edition Inc. Since the flamingo logo was his idea and he's the one out on the road for what he describes as a very small family company, I asked him why he wasn't president yet.

"Dad wanted to be president. How are you going to turn your own dad down when he says he wants to be president? Besides, he's putting up most of the money."

Oh.

If the flamingo logo idea works out, and I personally don't see how in heck it could ever fail, the Callaways will cash in. We aren't talking blue light specials here, David explains. The flamingo is emblazoned on a 100 percent cotton shirt, made in the USA, which will retail in the $35 to $40 range.

As soon as all the fancy designers find out that flamingo wear is on the market, they'll soon be crying in their aperitifs.

Bye bye, Izod. See ya later, alligator.

A Bird of the Ages

To those scoffers who mock Florida's only native art form and say the noble flamingo is only a fad and a fanciful frippery, I say Pffaugh! and give you the back of my hand.

The yardbirds which grace so many lawns in this part of Florida have a pedigree which goes back beyond even my wildest imaginings. I mean, can you envision the possibility of yard flamingos planted along Hadrian's Wall or beautifying the Forum or the Appian Way?

You probably can't, and I couldn't either until enlightenment came last week.

You can imagine how excited I got when a fellow employee here at the Little Miracle of Sixth Street dropped by my desk to say he has discovered major interest in the flamingo a century before the time of Christ.

It's information such as this which will cement this column's position as the leading defender and exponent of Florida yard statuary. I am quietly proud.

Imagine, in this coin collector's possession is a denarius minted by Fabius Hadrianus in 102 B.C. One side (I think it's the obverse, but I never could get the obverse and reverse thing straight — it's sorta like stalagtites and stalagmites, (y'know what I mean?) features a bust of Cybele wearing a turreted crown and veil.

The other side is of Victory holding the reins of a team of prancing horses. Beneath the team of horses is a bird.

193

Okay, some of the reference books such as Sydenham's Coinage of the Roman Republic and Seaby's Roman Silver Coins talk trash about this bird being a stork or a hawk.

But I throw my support behind Michael H. Crawford, a lecturer in ancient history at the University of Cambridge. In his tome, Roman Republican Coinage I, Crawford makes the flamingo connection.

And I'm sure all right-thinking numismatists and dealers in antiquuities will agree with my strong support of the Crawford thesis.

If the bird were only a mere stork, the coin wouldn't command the high price it does today. These babies go for more than 200 bucks apiece, and I'd never pay that unless I was assured of getting a genuine flamingo.

See? Sheer proof.

I wanted to run a picture of this find, which I have dubbed "Flamingus Denarius," but the coin is so small and the detail so fine that we weren't able to get a print of publishable quality.

But I was fortunate enough to view the coin and I was impressed. Trust me. Would I lie to you?

My beloved pink yard ornament truly is the Bird of the Ages.

Flamingophiles Bust Feathers over New Logo

Dontcha just love it? I mean, the news from Tallahassee Monday about the new symbol for the Florida State Lottery?

The design, selected from a field of 50 candidates, was a neat logo featuring a golden Sun and a pink, sort of, flamingo. My phone was ringing off the hook and co-workers dropped by the desk to ask if moi had anything to do with the selection.

Even though this column has been the staunchest defender of Florida's only native art form, the yard flamingo, for years, I can't take credit for this outstanding turn of events. And you know I would if I could, you understand.

I called Tallahassee (providing once again we spare no expense to bring you the latest yardbird happenings) and discovered the genius behind this logo is Judy Rutz, an artist with the Governor's Graphics Department.

Judy won this ole Cracker's heart right off when I asked her where she was from. "I'm proud to say I'm a Florida native," she spoke right up. Turns out she was born and raised in West Palm Beach, then became one of those Florida Gators up in Gainesville and now lives in the state capital.

I should send her a yard flamingo, because she says up to now her house doesn't boast any flamingobilia, but maybe that will change after the world finds out she's been inducted into the prestigious Sunday Punch Fabulous Friends of the Florida Flamingo Club.

She does, however, have a friend who is flat ate up with flamingo fever and owns a trove of souvenirs and consulted the friend's collection before coming up with the winning lottery logo.

What I like most about Judy is that she showed proper reverence for the 'mingo motif. She rejected some of the cartoon images and frivolous drawings of yardbirds for a more dignified approach.

Aware that many tourists and residents associate Florida with flamingos, she observed: "I showed respect for the flamingo. I used it as a graphic symbol."

Way to go, Judy. I think the flamingo logo is an odds-on favorite and a sure thing.

Now contrast the bright and positive comments from Judy with the negative natterings of some guy from Fort Myers who not only doesn't cotton to the new logo but seems to be in the throes of some kind of phobia.

The Fort Myers critic complains that the bird isn't indigenous to Florida. *"The flamingo,"* he harumphs, *"is a false image."*

But nothing can stop the flamingo juggernaut now. People are thinking pink to a fare-thee-well and all get-out. In fact, my flamingo news and views from across the Southeast basket runneth over and I'll have to give you all the other neat stuff next Sunday, including some startling news from Miami, great tourist trash from the side of the highway in South Carolina and a couple of Flagler Beach restaurateurs who have caught the wave.

Stay tuned.

Florida's lottery ticket "mingo."

Flamingo Moratorim
Finally over

Hee hee. You have fallen into my trap. For weeks, yea even months, I have purposely avoided mention of Florida's only native art form in these pages while my group of conspirators met in a small storefront office at 118 Madison Avenue and made our plans.

Hooray. Hooray. The first of May. Flamingo publicity begins today.

It will culminate in a gala May 14 celebration at Riverfront Park in Daytona Beach we have dubbed the Flamingo Fun Fair. (Blush) (Shuffle of feet) (hands folded in front in the fig leaf stance) (head kind of down in the "Aw shucks" mode) Yours truly is the ornery chairman of the big doin's.

That's not the important part. The folks who are doing the hard work are the volunteer coordinators and a whole bunch of other neat folks who support the local chapter of the Alzheimer's Disease Association.

To give you an idea of the kind of firepower for flamingos this fair will boast, let me drop a couple of names. Our auctioneer is my good ole buddy and the area's number one toastmaster, Bert Reames. I'm also cooking up an amazing deal with Congersman Bill Chappell.

It's hard to be humble when you have a leadership position in the promulgation of knowledge about the noble yard flamingo. We're going to have a passel of fun on May 14 from 9 a.m. to 6 p.m. I'm giving Bert a real jewel to auction off to the highest bidder. Bring lots of money because this won't go cheap.

It's a padded toilet seat with an embroidered flamingo on the cover. Yep, we're going to auction it off, still in its original plastic wrapper.

First on the schedule will be a flamingo costume contest, with $50 savings bonds to the champs, plus fairgoers can browse among the arts and crafts which honor the flamingo image and much more.

Later, there will be dancing (but not by me), folk music, magic shows, clowns and lots of foolishness (which I specialize in). I'm going to preach about the Flamingo Fun Fair again next week, but I wanted you to know about it now so as to mark your May calendars.

If any of you other flamingophiles out there want to contribute a suitably pink item for Bert to auction off for charity, let us know. We need all the help we can get because this is the first ever flamingo fair and, t' tell the truth, we are not exactly positive we know what we're doing.

But, naturally, that never has stopped me before so it's full steam ahead for flamingo power. It's time again to think pink.

Once Again, We Celebrate Florida's Yard Flamingos

I did the best I could. My intentions were pure. In this incarnation of the Sunday Punch column, I had hoped to liberate me, and you, from a topic that dominated the first string of Punch columns from 1984-91.

But everywhere I go, the same question comes up.

"When are you going to write about yard flamingos?"

Letters and cards on the subject have poured in. In fact, a card just poured in last week.

Be careful what you wish for, you might get it. The flamingo columns in this space set off the most shameful chapter of self promotion, bad taste, ethics violations, pandering to the lowest common denominator, manipulativeness and misdirected humor in the annals of journalism.

Maybe that explains why I loved it so much.

When I was invited by my beloved editor to resume writing Sunday Punch, I briefly considered making it a no-flamingo zone. Silly me. I vastly underestimated the strength of the forces I had unwittingly unleashed almost a decade ago.

Pink power reigns supreme. The 4-F Club I founded, the redoubtable Fabulous Friends of the Florida Flamingo, still flocks together. (Or we shall surely flock separately.)

How did it all happen? I forgot until I went back into the musty archives and found the first blatantly pro-flamingo column I ever

199

wrote. It was May 4, 1986, a day that will forever live in infamy. . . .

Oh sure, I had mentioned yard flamingos before then, but never with the high dudgeon exhibited on this date. What got me all pink in the face was a front page headline over a photo of a yard flamingo in The News-Journal that week. The headline was "Vogue Tackiness."

Well, tacky is as tacky does. I was nonplused. I was replete with rue. I mounted a stirring defense, pointing out that yard flamingos were Florida's only native art form.

Not all of my argument was emotional. I mixed in a few facts, just to keep my enemies off balance. I wrote: *"A society which does not prize lawn statuary is doomed. At their heights, Greece and Rome excelled in the production of lawn ornamentation. But have you noticed that most of the garden statues in those countries are weathered, broken or in disrepair?*

"And they aren't world powers any more either. Coincidence or what?"

And later, I carried on, waxing pretty eloquently for a guy who won't even wax his pickup truck. . . .

"Think Pink. Pinkspeace. 'Mingo Power. Yay for the Yardbirds!"

And in conclusion: *"If it were left to me to choose a government without flamingos or flamingos without government, I would unhesitatingly choose the latter. Love me, love my 'mingos. I used to feel sorry for myself because I had no class, but then I met a man who had no flamingos.*

"I'm pink, therefore I am. When flamingos are outlawed, only outlaws will have flamingos."

I shouldn't have been so pinkly passionate. The floodgates opened, and I was up to my you-know-what in flamingos in no time. I could have opened a beachside gift shop.

About that time, I asked my esteemed publisher if he would consider placing all the pink donations in a display case in The News-Journal lobby for all to see. He laughed and said something under his breath, I don't know what it was. I didn't get the display case, so I displayed most of the ill-gotten gain at my desk.

The mingomania went on unabated. I received flamingo memo pads, pencils, bedroom slippers, swizzle sticks and, my personal favorite, refrigerator magnets. (I consider a note anchored by a refrigerator magnet one of the most important methods of communication between parents and children.)

A group of gifted sixth-graders at Tomoka Elementary gave me a fuzzy little flamingo doll named Friday. A friend who was working for Burdine's, contributed a (I'm not making this up) flamingo toilet seat.

Another friend then created one of the most unusual biker T-shirts I've ever seen. It featured a growling 'mingo in leather and boots as a Bike Week promotion for the Boot Hill Saloon, which he owned at the time. The shirt became an instant hit with the London Symphony Orchestra, which was here that year, so in a way, this column has inspired many cultural crosscurrents.

Sorta like what would happen if Luciano Pavarotti started hangin' with Hank Willliams Jr.

I don't know if we are ready for more of that kind of jarring culture shock. I held off writing about flamingos as long as I could. The way I figure it, whatever happens now is your own dern fault. . . . Don't say you weren't warned.

Is It Time for a Pink Flamingo Club Revival?

"There is a tide in the affairs of men, which, taken at the flood, leads on to fortune."

Ole Brutus his own se'f said that, or at least Willie Shakespeare said he said it. Of course, what Brutus didn't know at the time was that the tides were about to turn against him big time. I'm a believer that there are such tides. In sports jargon, it's known as momentum or a basketball player could call it being "in the zone."

Gamblers go on a roll. Baseball players have streaks. To NASCAR drivers it's "just wunna them deals."

Anyhow, I've been on this unconscious run in the last few weeks that just as I sit down to put my Sunday chat with you in writing, you readers come to the rescue.

Truth is, there is no telling what you might be reading right now were it not for those bodacious tides of men.

I strolled into the newsroom one day last week to take one of my 30-minute work breaks when I saw an envelope sitting on my desk. I recognized the handwriting.

Once before, this anonymous benefactor has left interesting notes for me. Maybe sometime this secret benefactor will uncloak and I can give proper credit.

The envelope was thick, and I opened it to find a cassette tape and a sheet of lyrics. The note said: *"Sir."* (A clue! Must be somebody who doesn't know me.) *"Knowing of your love for flamingos, I thought you might find this song appropriate.*" It is signed "A Regular Reader." (Which I suppose eliminates all you irregular readers out there from suspicion.)

Anyhow, the words to this tune make it sorta the National Anthem of Spam-suckin' trailer trash, the likes of which you see on Maury, Montel or Oprah. I will spare you the verses, because all the great flamingo stuff is in the title and the chorus. It's called (Ta-DAAA) *"Pink Flamingos"* and the chorus goes like this:

"We got pink flamingos in the front yard
Picture window with a view of Wal-Mart
Blue collar heaven . . . domestic bliss
It just don't get any better than this.
We got pink flamingos, pink flamingos, pink flamingos."

Kinda gets you right here, don't it?

I'm on the verge of giving in to this pink tide. Might as well go with the flow.

We may be well on the cutting edge of a revival of pinkpower as we know it. When flamingos are outlawed, only outlaws will have flamingos.

Did Yard Flamingos Migrate from Massachusetts?

I caught the pink tide of flamingo fortune just before it began to crest in the 1980s. Veteran Sunday readers know that I worked my head to the bone to keep up with the latest in 'mingo madness during that time.

But a couple of years ago, I decided the fad had run its course and I would downplay the noble yardbird. I thought it was time to let the flamingo quietly assume its rightful place in the pop culture hall of fame.

Wrong!

Another wave of 'Mingo Mania maybe about to crest. I don't know if it's the phase of the moon or what, but the pink birds have been much in evidence this past week.

I walked into the Little Miracle of Sixth Street one day last week only to find a fellow employee waiting with a grin and a clipping from the Noo Yawek Times its own se'f in her hand.

The article was about a company that rents displays of pink plastic flamingos for special occasions. It makes the claim that the plastic yard flamingo was first created and marketed by Union Products of Leominster, Massachusetts, in 1956.

That may be true, but I remember concrete ones in Florida yards long before that.

As if that wasn't enough, another copy of the clipping arrived in the mail Friday courtesy of a friend living in DeLand.

"Something seems amis," she wrote.

Well, too much ain't enough. Another DeLandite sent me another article about the Leominster legend. This one was printed in Yankee Magazine.

The article says Union Products now sells about a quarter of a million of the yardbirds a year.

"It's become the national backyard bird," said Don Featherstone, the inventor.

Sorry, Don, but I have pretty low regard for anyone who hides yard flamingos in the back yard. Front yard and proud, I say.

According to Don, his best customer was a guy in Guilford, Connecticut, who has 400 in his yard. Some guy in Alaska bought a few dozen and marooned them on an ice floe in the Arctic Ocean to see where they would end up.

They haven't been seen since.

So that's how it all came about that I'm writing about flamingo stuff today.

This may represent another groundswell of pinkpower as we know it. Who knows, I may even have to resurrect the ol' Fabulous Friends of the Florida Flamingo, or 4-F Club.

Stay tuned, boys and girls.

Leominster's Claim
to Fame Losing Appeal

I've never been to Leominster, but I guess that someday I should make a pilgrimage to that small Central Massachusetts community.

Like a half-remembered melody that won't leave your mind, Leominster has been a recurring name in the ole mailbag since the mid-1980s, when I penned my first column on Florida's only native art form, the yard flamingo.

Pronounced "LEM-in-ster," this New England municipality is the home of Don Featherstone, hailed as the inventor of the pink plastic yard flamingo; his company, Union Products Inc.; and the esteemed National Plastics Center and Museum.

Union Products sells about 250,000 yardbirds a year and up to 20 million have been sold since Featherstone created the fad more than 40 years ago.

"It's become the national backyard bird," Featherstone boasts. And he gets really defensive if anyone dares suggest the dreaded T- word in describing the noble birds.

"People say they're tacky, but all great art began as tacky," said the inventor, whose signature is molded into every plastic 'mingo body.

But pinkpower is not the real theme of today's offering. There is more big news in Leominster having to do with the town's other main claim to fame.

It's the birthplace of John Chapman, the man most of us know and love as "Johnny Appleseed."

Chapman was born September 26, 1774, in Leominster and died in Fort Wayne, Indiana, on March 18, 1845. He did not simply stroll down frontier roads strewing apple seeds, as some stories claim, but was a very skilled and dedicated nurseryman.

He not only planted individual trees, but orchards and plant nurseries across the Midwest, which then was America's wild frontier. He also planted medicinal herbs, believing that his contributions would provide food and comfort for pioneer families.

His contribution was not haphazard. He often returned to prune and care for trees in the orchards and nurseries he had created.

Leominster had not made much of its Johnny Appleseed connection until a few years ago, when local politicians and businessmen decided it had marketing appeal.

Today, Mayor Dean Mazzarella and some other Leominster leading lights are aghast. It seems the owner of Sholan Farms, the city's last working apple orchard, has decided to get out of the fruit business and into big-time development.

The owner wants to convert the 50 acres of apple trees and the farm's cupola-capped barn into a subdivision boasting 161 four-bedroom homes.

Similar housing developments are already perched on land that once provided vistas of fruit-laden trees and grazing cows. The financial incentive for development is quite strong, with many new homes in the area carrying $350,000 price tags.

Town fathers hope to collect the millions of dollars needed to save the orchard. On the city's Internet Web page is an exciting new development, breathlessly reported by His Honor.

"Mayor Mazzarella is pleased to announce that he is entering into a partnership with Wicky Wax Candle Shop to raise money to purchase Sholan Farms. Sholan Farms Baked Apple, the first candle in the Mayor Mazzarella Collection, will sell for $10.00 each. For every candle sold, $4.00 will go towards the purchase of Sholan Farms."

Stay tuned, folks. It'll be interesting to see if anyone can hold a candle to this fund drive, which it could be said, is the apple of the mayor's eye.

Cities' Pride Links Florida and New England

Last week, this column outlined the efforts of Mayor Dean Mazzarella and other Leominster, Massachusetts, worthies to save the town's last remaining apple orchard from the developer's bulldozer.

The town takes great pride in the fact the John Chapman, known better to most of us as "Johnny Appleseed," was born there.

Also thrown in was some history that many of you veteran readers recall very well, that Leominster is credited as the birthplace of the pink plastic yard flamingo about 41 years ago.

It seems that many of you sent copies of last week's column to Mayor Mazzarella.

I have no way of knowing how popular His Honor is up there in the appleseed and plastic 'mingo capital of the world, but I can tell you that if I lived there, he would get my vote.

He's quite an eloquent spokesman for his city, and has issued me a cordial invitation to visit Leominster in the near future. Well, what can I say? I have accepted, though I don't know exactly when I'll be able to drop by.

Rest assured that when I do, it will be reported here in your favorite Sunday mullet wrapper.

The Mayor also communicated some astonishing news about his city's history.

You know, us Carters don't get a lot of respect in these parts. We are looked upon as a kind of low class. A rich Carter is a guy with TWO old cars up on blocks in his front yard. Carters are very puzzled about such cultural things as ballet dancing. We just wonder why they don't hire taller girls.

But up in Leominster, I'm going to be a big deal, and maybe a descendant of some very well-educated town fathers.

Mayor Mazzarella told me that Carters have infiltrated right smart up there. Leominster boasts a Carter Street, a Carter park and even a Carter junior high school.

Four Carter brothers, Nathaniel, Jonathan, Oliver and Josiah, were among the first to settle the area in 1735.

There is a historical marker on a place called Carter Hill (This is getting really good!) in memory on one of the sons of a Captain James Carter, who sired 11 children, one being James Gordon Carter.

James Gordon Carter attended Groton Academy and Harvard University, then became one of the state's most influential educational reformers, founding three normal schools for teacher training. And in 1837, he drafted the bill that established the board of education.

Now, I hope this silences some of you carping critics out there. I am quietly proud.

"I used to feel sorry for myself because I had no class, but then I met a man who had no flamingos."

— *JC*

Writings Recalled

John was both a voracious reader and an involved reader. He was always searching for a new favorite book. Once a book touched him, he would become its advocate, salesman and defender. "A Confederacy of Dunces" and "Catch-22" topped his charts the longest. He had multiple copies of both so they could always be given to fellow readers. You could not ignore a Carter reading recommendation.

— ML

Cross Creek

"It seems to me that the earth may be borrowed but not bought. It may be used but not owned. It gives itself in response to love and tending, offers its seasonal flowering and fruiting. But we are tenants and not possessors, lovers and not masters. Cross Creek belongs to the wind and the rain, to the sun and the seasons, to the cosmic secrecy of seed, and beyond all, to time."

The lady who wrote those beautiful lines is buried in Antioch Cemetery, near Island Grove. Marjorie Kinnan Rawlings was not a Florida native, but few lives were more intertwined with our beautiful land of flowers than hers.

You know her as the Pulitzer Prize-winning author of "The Yearling," and of other acclaimed books such as "South Moon Under" and "Cross Creek," from which the above quote was taken.

Only 50 feet away in another Antioch Cemetery plot lie the last remains of Zelma Cason. Together in death, they had been grand antagonists in life.

Florida natives consider an outsider to be an outsider forever. No matter how well a Yankee assimilates, there is always an invisible line which can't be crossed.

Marjorie Kinnan Rawlings made the mistake of putting Zelma Cason in "Cross Creek." It's believed that Rawlings received verbal permission from all of her neighbors portrayed in the book, including Zelma, but nothing was put in writing.

One can only imagine the shockwaves that reverberated through the tiny Cross Creek community once Zelma eagerly took up her copy of "Cross Creek" to read about herself.

She found this: *"Zelma is an ageless spinster resembling an angry and efficient canary."* There are also claims that Cason was prone to profanity.

Zelma Cason sued, charging the author with invasion of privacy.

Sounds laughable, but the case actually dragged on until it cost Rawlings about $32,000 in legal fees. Turns out it broke new legal turf in Florida as the first case ever to pit privacy rights against freedom of speech rights.

In 1946, Rawlings took the stand in a Gainesville circuit courtroom to defend herself. "I felt I had come home when I came to Florida," she testified. "The people so charmed me I determined to write about them and, if I failed, not to write anymore."

Rawlings won that case, but the vengeful Zelma appealed to the Florida Supreme Court. The supremes reversed the decision, awarding Zelma $1 in damages.

Both sides lost. Zelma got one miserable buck and Rawlings was brought so low she never wrote about Florida and her neighbors again.

That's a shame, because I'm one fifth-generation Floridian who would have been proud to have Rawlings write about me, even if she called me a jug-eared kid or a gray-haired curmudgeon.

She also redeemed herself with her neighbors many times over by helping the tiny Cross Creek community of State Road 325 fight the growth monster.

Those were crucial times to be fighting growth too, because the developers pretty much raped, pillaged and burned Florida between the Great Depression and the day Rawlings died up in Crescent Beach in 1953.

If the great lady had lived, we would be celebrating her 100th birthday this year.

Her Cross Creek home, a state and national historical treasure, reopened for tours this week, The grove, nature trail and yard around the house are open every day for leisurely strolls, but the guided tours of the home have a much more restricted schedule, though peeking through the windows is always allowed.

The house is closed Mondays, Tuesdays and Wednesdays and all month during August and September for repairs and restoration work.

There is a small admission charge and tours are limited to groups of 10.

The ole Cracker highly recommends the tour for everybody who is a Florida native or those who, just like Marjorie Kinnan Rawlings her own se'f, want to be.

Letters Offer Glimpse into Author Hurston's Heart

Last week's ramblings about Cross Creek and Marjorie Kinnan Rawlings set my mind to wandering about another great author, a contemporary and friend of Rawlings, who also helped preserve the customs and tall tales of rural Florida.

In November 1989, my learned friend Steve Glassman put on a series of seminars at Embry-Riddle Aeronautical University honoring the life and work of Zora Neale Hurston.

I owe Steve a great debt for introducing me to Zora and her writings.

Though Zora was one of the leading lights in the Harlem Renaissance literary and social movement, her roots were firmly planted in Florida. She was born in Florida, the daughter of the mayor of Eatonville, a black enclave of Orlando. She died in Florida, her remains now resting in a small Fort Pierce cemetery.

Rawlings wrote "Cross Creek" and "The Yearling," and Hurston authored "Jonah's Gourd Vine," "Mules and Men" and "Seraph on the Suwanee." Both writers showed a remakable sensitivity toward both blacks and whites struggling to eke out lives in rural Florida.

It's not a great leap of logic to say that they were among the first to explore the common bond linking the poor of all races and show in an oblique way that racial prejudice was only a ploy to divide and subjugate them.

When Zora was earning her anthopology degree from Barnard

216

College, she could have selected some of the leading literary and musical lions of her generation as a topic.

That includes Jacksonville's notable native son, James Weldon Johnson, Countee Cullen, Claude McKay and Langston Hughes.

Instead, she went to Florida piney woods turpentine camps to listen to the songs and stories of the workers. Or she surveyed her friends and relatives in Eatonville.

Once I listened to an audio tape of Zora's own voice singing some of the turpentine camp songs she collected. Some of them were too raw to be printed in this newspaper, but Zora unblushingly added those to her list.

One of her "finds" was a folk tune called "Mule on the Mountain" which has at least 40 known verses and is believed to be the longest song commonly sung in America.

With their love and respect for the common man, I'm not a bit surprised that Marjorie and Zora became friends and often corresponded. While researching a feature story on the local Zora Conference, I came across some of that correspondence.

Zora was living in a houseboat on the Halifax River in 1943. She came here for rest and a recharging of her intellectual batteries.

Life was good in her Halifax houseboat days, and Zora by all accounts was an enthusiastic and accomplished letter writer, a skill to be highly prized because so few are good at it.

Last week, I shared with you a beautiful sample of Marjorie's writing. Today, I have a similar offering from Zora's heart.

These were written about 1943 and are excerpts from her letters to her colleague in letters:

She affectionately described her small houseboat and once invited Rawlings over for a visit. But, she playfully warned, the galley was small and the even smaller toilet was one which visitors could use *"only if your behind doesn't stick out too far."*

In another letter: Zora boasted that she had *"achieved one of my life's pleasures by owning at last a houseboat. Nothing to delay the sun in its course. The Halifax River is very beautiful and the various natural expressions of the day on the river keep me happier than I have ever been before in my life. Here I can forget for short periods the greed and brutality of man to man."*

217

And another letter, which I admire for its lyrical ending:

"I have the solitude that I love. All the other boat owners are very nice to me. Not a word about race. I love the sunshine the way it is done in Florida. Rain the same way — in great slews or not at all. I dislike the cold weather and its kinfolk: That takes in bare trees and a birdless morning."

'Explanation' Key to Keeping Friendship Alive

If you recall your high school civics lessons, John Adams and Thomas Jefferson were very unlikely friends. Though united in their passion to create a new nation, they quickly took different paths and became intense political rivals.

Geography, religion and politics formed what seemed an insurmountable gulf.

Adams snubbed Jefferson at the latter's inauguration, and left behind the last-minute appointment of political cronies in federal posts across the young nation. Jefferson undid Adams' mischief, but then wrote many injudicious remarks about his fellow warrior in the vineyards of democracy, some of which fell into the wrong hands and were printed.

A 12-year period elapsed in which the two old friends ignored each other, with only an occasional contact through third parties.

The rift was finally ended, not by the southern patrician Jefferson, but by the fiery Adams. His conciliatory line in his first direct letter to Jefferson after more than a decade is, to me, one of the greatest and most poignant invitations to further correspondence ever written. These short words never fail to move and inspire me.

"You and I ought not to die," Adams wrote simply, *"before we have explained ourselves to each other."*

The flood of letters which ensued, some 155 of them, became the heart of what Jefferson himself once termed "A Republic of Letters"

219

and a time historians term the "golden age of letter writing in America and England."

The Adams-Jefferson letters were only part of a massive collection of papers and correspondence. Historians say the Herculean task of identifying, cataloging and printing their complete works will run into the middle of the 21st century.

Jefferson broke his wrist in a fall and was likely crippled by what we know now as carpal tunnel syndrome, but even to the end, his letters were works of art. Adams suffered from palsy for the last few years of his life and was forced at times to dictate his letters.

But nothing stopped these two old friends from exchanging their views on the great issues of the day, and nearly always ending with an expression of love and regard for each other.

On Independence Day of 1826, Jefferson was invited to attend a celebration in Washington. Adams was invited to similar events in Washington, Philadelphia and New York. Both were on their death beds and could not attend.

On that July 4th the 50th anniversary of the founding of our Republic, John Adams died at about 5 o'clock in the afternoon. His dying words were a tribute to his sometimes enemy and always friend: "Thomas Jefferson survives."

If anyone had written this as fiction, no one would believe it. I hope that it might become for you, as it has to me, an inspiration the next time you feel too tired to write someone you love.

And it leads me to ask if there is an old friend out there, and somehow over the years you have fallen apart, or you go mad at each other for some slight, real or imagined.

You could do worse than to take out pen and paper, and begin by writing, say, something like *"You and I ought not to die before we have explained ourselves to each other."*

Fond Memories of
Down-to-Earth Winner

This is my fourth try at coming up with a lead for this column, and I'm thinking about junking it, too. I think Robert Lewis Taylor would know what I'm talking about, since he viewed writing, as I do, as a trade and not an art.

It's actually work, more akin to plumbing and ditch-digging than communing with the Muse.

I only had a couple of long conversations with Taylor back in 1978, and I never heard from him again. But for some strange reason, I always counted him as a friend and a fellow laborer in the vineyards of vocabulary.

Then, when I was researching a column I discovered Taylor died about three months before at his Connecticut home.

"Novelist and biographer Robert Lewis Taylor dies at age 88" was one headline. Another one I found said: *"Robert Lewis Taylor, at 88, wrote for The New Yorker."*

For the record, Taylor was born in Carbondale, Illinois, where he took his first job as a reporter for the local paper. He left after a year and jumped a steamer to Tahiti, where he stayed until he ran out of money and had to come back to the United States to work for the St. Louis Post-Dispatch, a paper identified with the Pulitzer Prize.

That's important, because in 1959, Taylor won a Pulitzer for "The Travels of Jaimie McPheeters," a novel about the glory days of the California Gold Rush.

He also attracted notice for his witty New Yorker articles and for biographies of Carry Nations, W.C. Fields and Winston Churchill.

His 1961 novel, "A Journey to Matecumbe," was rewritten into a screenplay for the 1976 Disney flick "Treasure of Matecumbe."

In 1978, Taylor and his wife were spending part of the year in a Daytona Beach Shores condo, where I was invited for lunch a couple of times and for long conversations about writing. I especially recall his words about the Prize.

"I've thought very seriously of having it carved on my tombstone," he said with a laugh. "It follows me along sort of like a kite tail. Don't get me wrong, I'm grateful for the award, but it annoys me that it gives a cachet to a book that it doesn't quite deserve."

Taylor was an accomplished storyteller who regaled me with funny stories about partying with W.C. Fields and being outsmarted by Winston Churchill.

My favorite was his narrative on how he once contacted Churchill's staff to ask for an interview and for the old man's blessing on his book.

After many weeks of cajoling and scheming, Taylor was granted an audience. At noon, Taylor was ushered into Churchill's bedroom. The prime minister was propped up in bed breakfasting on a whole baked chicken, a bottle of white wine and two highballs. "He had his glasses down on his nose, like this," Taylor said, pantomiming the scene.

The great man refused to acknowledge the writer's presence for a long time. Taylor stood there, shifting his weight from one foot to the other. Finally, Churchill looked up and croaked: "Young man . . . any money that is to be made from writing about my life, I hope to make myself."

Interview over.

I recalled that story when I read a gossip item this week claiming that Hillary Rodham Clinton had refused to cooperate in a planned biography of her life to be penned by famed Watergate journalist Carl Bernstein. Someone on Mrs. Clinton's staff reportedly said that no one was as qualified to write about the first lady as the first lady her own self.

That started me rummaging around for my files on Robert Lewis Taylor and led to the sad information about his death.

You don't have to take off your shoes to count the hours I actually spent talking with Taylor, but he was one of the most fascinating persons I've ever interviewed.

After all, is there anyone you know who ever quit his job and hopped a tramp steamer to the South Pacific to get drunk with W.C. Fields? I rest my case.

Poem's Inspiration Is
Worth Bending Rules

I've always been a big believer in breaking rules, and there's one that I've broken twice in recent Sunday columns. It's not the regular policy of your friendly hometown newspaper to run poetry in its pages, especially the homemade stuff which almost everybody hides in a notebook underneath their underwear in the dresser drawer.

So some of my colleagues were surprised when they saw I had defied the informal ban on rhyme a couple of Sunday's ago, praising the noble flamingo.

In those columns were excerpts from poems composed by two certified holders of the coveted pink feather denoting them as Fabulous Friends of the Florida Flamingo, or as we call it in the newsroom, the 4-F Club.

This discussion of poetry reminds me of a wonderful conversation I had almost a decade ago with our late editor and publisher, Herbert M. Davidson. It was a quiet Saturday and HMD decided to share some of his knowledge and insights about the news biz with me.

I asked why we had an aversion to running verse in the newspaper. HMD fixed me with an unblinking gaze and said firmly: "There's a lot of bad poetry out there, John."

This prologue is all leading up to a story I'm about to tell which is going to cause me to violate our policy a third time. Yep, this column is gonna close with a smidgen of poetry.

About a baker's dozen years ago, I was mired in what most would agree is a down cycle. Freshly divorced, out of work, in debt by several thousand dollars and spending what little money I had left on my three-pack-a-day cigarette habit and as much beer as I could put on a tab at the neighborhood bar.

I went with a friend to what probably is the world's largest flea market — known as "First Monday" in Canton, Texas. As I strolled along the booths, I found a grizzled old timer etching little sayings and bits of poems on pieces of metal or wood.

He was a fascinating person, and we chatted for about an hour. My financial position wasn't too hot. A hot dog and a soft drink I purchased earlier had left less than two bucks in change in my pockets. But the old timer took my meager pieces of silver in exchange for what he said was his favorite bit of verse, one he guaranteed had stood the test of time.

He never said who wrote it and I didn't ask. I took the copper-colored etched plate home and put it on the wall.

As I gradually dug myself out of the financial and emotional depths, there were many times that the inscription comforted and encouraged me. Just before I left Texas and returned to my native Florida, I had a friend going through a similar crisis, except she also was burdened by a child whose behavior at home and school was breaking her heart and threatening her ability to keep her job at the bowling alley.

I gave her the little etched plaque. A few years later, she said that she passed it on to a friend who was suffering through a health crisis.

I have no idea if the circle is unbroken, but I fantasize sometimes that the little plaque is still circulating somewhere, uplifting spirits and inspiring survival skills.

So my little Sunday gift to you this week is that little bit of poetry, which I found after much digging and research in the library was taken from a work titled "Ulysses" by Alfred, Lord Tennyson.

We are not now that strength which in old days
Moved earth and heaven, that which we are, we are—
One equal temper of heroic hearts,
Made weak by time and fate, but strong in will
To strive, to seek, to find and not to yield.

John and daughter Karen, silhouetted against Lake Okeechobee.

Convictions

. . . (he) knew that what truly separates man from the animals is the capacity to stand divided against itself. Time and time again he bore this conflict up to us bravely and shone before us in his nakedness. Often we thought this humbled him when it was we, ourselves, who should have been humbled."

—JC

Holocaust Survivor Spent Life Fighting Evil

Adolf Hitler wanted Senta Gerstein to die a meaningless, shameful and early death.

Instead, against all odds, she outlived her nemesis by more than four decades and created a new life of achievement, love and indomitable spirit that brought her victory over all the hellish forces of Nazi Germany.

Death finally claimed Senta's great and good heart last Monday, and all week I have been filled to overflowing with the mixed emotions of sadness at the Daytona Beach resident's passing and the exhilaration of her lifetime triumph over evil.

When Senta was a child in Hamburg, Germany, women were not encouraged to excel. But she was a dynamo not to be denied. Senta was a scholar in art, literature, history and philosophy at the University of Hamburg. She learned Jewish history, ethics and faith at the feet of the chief rabbi in Hamburg.

Her brilliance as a writer and lecturer naturally attracted attention. She was forced to obtain a permit issued by the Gestapo, and a Gestapo agent was assigned to shadow her on lecture tours.

Senta was the star of a regular radio program in which she told fairy tales and other children's stories. The broadcasts were monitored to make sure she was not sneaking subversive information into her tales.

While the Nazis were trying to find hidden messages in her radio fairy tales, Senta was playing a dangerous game as a secret messenger for a network of German Jews, using the lecture tours as cover.

When many of her relatives and friends disappeared, Senta rightly assumed she must escape quickly or face a similar fate. (Only 900 of the 22,000 Jews in Hamburg survived.) She was placed on a train bound for the Netherlands where further arrangements would be made for her escape.

There was a terrifying three-hour interrogation by SS officers at the border and another several hours when Senta was unconscious and did not remember what happened.

She ultimately made her way to New York, standing on the shores of the land of opportunity with nothing but the clothes she was wearing and a $5 bill, the amount given to arriving refugees.

"I gave up everything I was educated and trained for," she once told me. "It was a very hard struggle. I took odd jobs, physical work."

In a career that would sound like a Grade B movie plot if it weren't so real, Senta parlayed her $5 into a major fashion jewelry business in New York and Denver. She supervised 30 employees and distributed her jewelry, most of which she personally designed, in 36 states.

She and her husband Sol (also a Holocaust survivor) retired and came to Daytona Beach, but "retired" is a poor choice of words to describe Senta. She became a forceful advocate for a wide range of social issues. She lectured often and wrote an important reference text on those who lived with her in Hamburg from 1929 to 1939.

She championed the handicapped, homeless and unemployed. In 1976, then Governor Reubin Askew assigned her to do a survey on unemployment in Florida, and she was a recognized expert and innovator in programs to make life brighter and more humane for senior citizens, especially those in nursing homes.

At an Israel bonds rally here in 1983, she testified to what she had seen and experienced. With an authority that still impresses me, even as I think of it today, Senta recalled the unspeakable horror of the Holocaust: "It was the greatest devilish annihilation . . . 6 million dead, a figure incomprehensible in its enormity. Don't ask why, because there is no reply."

Then she concluded in triumph: "Doors closed. New gates opened. Human life never ceases to have meaning . . . the agonies of the Holocaust led to the sanctification of life."

Right Number

The voice on the telephone was soft, so low that I had to thumb the little dial on the handset to jack the audio up a couple of decibels. "I'd like to speak to the person who writes your Area News Briefs," she said politely.

I explained in my best businesslike tones that all reporters contribute these small but important items at some time or another. Assuming that this might be someone wanting a correction, I asked if I could help.

She explained that she was a recent rape victim, and the news account of her ordeal had been printed in one of our papers. She was hurt and confused about seeing the assault and robbery in print.

I fetched a back copy of the paper and read the news brief as the timid caller waited on the line. The story was fairly well written, crisp and to the point.

My mind shifted into overdrive and I had the quick, easy answer, the statement of our newsgathering policy ready to roll. I was ready to remind her that neither her name nor her address had been printed in the story and that her privacy had been protected. Why, I was even ready to quote the state public records law to her if necessary.

I was ready to do all of that, when I suddenly broke down. I didn't cry but I could feel my heart melting. Here was a woman who had suffered a terrible trauma and less than 48 hours later I was going to lay some pompous bureaucratic line on her. So what if my words were true. Who cares that they were to the point?

Rather than assault her with the truth, overwhelm her with facts and squelch her argument, I decided that I was on her side.

I took a chance that we usually fear to take with a stranger. For a moment, the departure from my quick, easy explanation turned me into a stammering idiot. "I'm not saying this well," I said correctly, "but I sympathize with you, my heart goes out to you. If there is anything in the story which offends you, I'm sorry."

Pretty lame, I guess for someone who prides himself in his use of words. But a miraculous moment crystallized. The roles reversed, and she responded sweetly, as if to comfort me for my lack of ability to say exactly the right thing.

My anonymous caller, the flesh and blood victim of the crime that now looked so cold printed in black and white next to my telephone, said that there wasn't anything specific that she wanted to correct in the article, it's just that it hurt to see the event mentioned in the newspaper.

Maybe, I replied, the description of her attacker will lead to his arrest. "I hope they get him," I continued, "and when they do I hope they won't let him off."

She said that she was hoping the same thing, and then worried aloud that maybe her description of the assailant wasn't complete enough to lead to an arrest. "I wasn't sure about the height, but I know I was right about the shoes. I'll never forget his shoes," she whispered.

There was a long pause. I think she mistook my silence as a rebuff, and she apologized for calling, for taking my time.

Fortunately, she was still on the line, so I could close by telling her that the call was welcome, that we did care about her perception of the article.

She said she was feeling a little better now that she had delivered her complaint, then said: "Thank you" in the same even, low voice and hung up.

In the next hour, I thought of all the sparkling, wonderful things I should have said. So, here is an open letter to my anonymous caller: This is what I wanted to say, but didn't.

"What happened to you is rotten and unfair, but it doesn't define who you are.

"If you have friends or relatives with whom you have a close bond, use them. If you feel the need to get help, don't be afraid to seek it.

"You are somebody, even if the Area News Briefs identified you only as a 'victim.' You were only a victim during the commission of a crime of violence. You weren't a victim before and you don't have to remain one now. You seem to be intelligent, caring and a decent person. It wasn't your fault. you can be victorious, even over this. We do care."

From Daytona Beach, She Moved the World

Doctor Mary McLeod Bethune, had we the good fortune to still have her with us, would have been 110 years old this week. That's reason enough to celebrate her achievements and reflect on the lessons of a life well spent, but this year is marked by two important community based movements.

A petition drive has begun to rename Second Avenue in her honor, and I can't dream of anyone who is more worthy or whose life has reflected such great credit on the Greater Daytona Beach Area as Mary McLeod Bethune. The second important event this week was an appeal for money by Bethune-Cookman College Student Government President Gregory Smith for restoration of the Bethune home, a national historic site.

I never met Mrs. Bethune but have eagerly listened to those in our community who were her friends, confidantes and proteges to the point I sometimes feel the power of her spirit. I have seen the college that this daughter of former slaves founded on a trash heap with only $1.50 in her purse.

Such was the force of Mary McLeod Bethune that the college is in more danger of failing today with its net worth of millions than it was in the days she kept it alive by sheer presence of will. What quaking of the knees, what mixture of awful responsibility and irresistible opportunity must have faced Dr. Richard V. Moore and Dr. Oswald Bronson the first days they sat in the president's chair as stewards of

Mrs. Bethune's legacy.

All private colleges and certainly all predominately black private schools are reeling under the onslaught of inflation and federal budget cuts in everything from student aid to faculty research grants.

B-CC is a community asset that deserves to be saved, and more than that, to prosper. I felt a chill during a speech on campus a couple of years ago by that talented man for all seasons, Choreographer, Painter and Raconteur Geoffrey Holder. "God Bless Mary McLeod Bethune," he shouted in that basso most profundo. "I feel as if I am on hallowed ground." Amen.

Recognition flowed to this magnetic and talented lady during her career, and Daytona Beach benefited from the spotlight. She was a trusted adviser to world leaders. President Franklin D. Roosevelt and his first lady Eleanor held special affection for this stalwart champion of minority and women's rights.

Governors, artists, writers, singers, educators and thousands of plain humble folk made pilgrimages to Daytona Beach to meet Mrs. Bethune. As her fame grew, the demands on her time took her to other states and nations, and she was a courageous spokesman for the rights of blacks and women when it took real gumption to do so.

These words sound as if they were uttered only a week ago, but Mary McLeod Bethune said them at a conference she organized under the theme "Women Can Lead The Way" in 1952. She said in the keynote speech: "Thinking women can send a voice that will penetrate to the ends of the Earth . . . I have called you together my beautiful women, that we may tune in together and create a great song that will vibrate around the World."

Oh, there were giants in those days, and it's rare when we find someone with the moral suasion and crystalline purity of purpose to produce oratory such as that and soften hardened hearts.

The name of a street and the preservation of a home is the minimum, a down payment, only a installment in the continuing debt the Greater Daytona Beach Area owes to such genius. Black and white must join with Nobel Laureate Dr. Ralph Bunche who counted it an honor just to stand beside Mary McLeod Bethune at B-CC's golden anniversary celebration in 1954 and proclaim her "one of the truly great personalities of the World."

Keeping a Commitment
to a Dream

"The woods are lovely dark and deep
But I have promises to keep
And miles to go before I sleep."

Robert Frost wrote those lines about a snow-covered forest in 1923, but he might just as well have been writing of the paradoxical mixture of nobility and imperfection, love and hate, that passes for modern-day race relations in this not-really-typical Southern town.

The imperfection and hate are mentioned to protect myself from charges that I'm a wimp or Pollyanna for writing what I'm about to: That this community did something in 1946 that makes us one of the most blessed and lucky places on the face of the Earth.

That is the year we became the "sanctuary" for the man who broke the color line in major-league baseball. And the good news is that we were handpicked as the site for that important task, because as bad as we were, we were light-years better than the competition.

In a spring training game at our local ballpark, Jackie Robinson faced major-league opposition for the first time. He played for the Montreal Royals in a game against the Brooklyn Dodgers, the Royals' parent club.

Though bigots in surrounding cities padlocked their ballparks rather than let Jackie perform, he found a welcome in Daytona Beach. Much of the credit goes to Mary McLeod Bethune and to the college she founded. The legacy of this great lady is the leaven that makes our

236

Daytona Beach what it is today and still is the catalyst for our most noble impulses.

And I'm proud of the place I work and am proud of the Davidson family, which displayed uncommon valor in the battle against racial injustice beginning with the day they took over this newspaper in 1928. No, that's not a misprint. We're talking about a commitment to civil rights that began at The News-Journal in, read my lips, Nineteen-TWENTY-eight.

I believe those factors and others inspired the Dodgers' Branch Rickey to select this city as the place to launch this great experiment.

That's all well and good, but what have we done lately? Glad you asked.

The city's image remains bright. We're quite a political science phenomenon, being a city that is two-thirds white and routinely votes two and sometimes three black leaders to its governing body, the City Commission. That commission, late last year, proved its continuing commitment to the legacy by naming our City Island ballfield for Jackie Robinson.

The commission renamed a major thoroughfare for Dr. Martin Luther King Jr. and a quiet campaign now is under way for similar honors in memory of the beloved Mrs. Bethune.

The News-Journal also remains committed to the dream. My boss, Tippen Davidson, has told me privately how pleased he is that the campaign to honor Jackie Robinson had it roots in a Chamber of Commerce Image Committee that he chaired a couple of years ago. A bright young radio newsman, Bill Schumann, served on that committee and has since worked tirelessly on the Jackie Robinson Memorial.

Schumann's energy in researching the project and in gaining the vital support of Rachel Robinson, Jackie's widow, and the foundation she heads have been applauded by many in the community.

There is a very low-key fund drive going on at present, but it will get high-key in the near future as Schumann and other area leaders get formally involved.

It's not really so much what it's going to do for Jackie Robinson, in a way. Jackie has his place in history, including enshrinement in baseball's Hall of Fame in Cooperstown, New York. The man will be revered for his trailblazing achievements in professional baseball.

But we have promises to keep to our brothers and sisters, black and white, and many miles to go before we can sleep. Thanks to good deeds done by an earlier generation of Daytonans, when we honor Jackie Robinson, we honor ourselves.

A 1997 photo of the Jackie Robinson Memorial at
Jackie Robinson Ballpark on City Island.

Passing the Torch
of Reason

To Monte Irvin, already 28 years old and beginning to wonder if he ever would get a chance at Big League baseball, it was "the perfect selection." Ed Charles, only 12 years old and beginning to wonder if he was going to have to go to reform school, marveled at "a spirit aflame."

Both of these comments, representing the impressions of both man and boy, honor Jackie Roosevelt Robinson, who broke the major-league baseball color line 40 years ago this season.

What makes that achievement even more wonderful is that Daytona Beach is an important part of the story.

Branch Rickey of the Brooklyn Dodgers carefully selected Daytona Beach as the place where Robinson would prepare himself for the ordeal of integrating our national pastime. That decision was quite a compliment to this city, and it was borne out by the rude reception Robinson received in Sanford, Jacksonville and elsewhere.

In later years, Robinson described this city as his "sanctuary," in contrast to the slurs hurled at him in some other places.

Our community wasn't perfect. For instance, Robinson was forced to stay in a private home because no motel would rent him a room. But the good will between the races engendered by Dr. Mary McLeod Bethune may have paid off. And the "back fence" friendships between white and black leaders who met in private to avoid the spite of local bigots may also have played a part.

239

Robinson and City Island Ballpark were the ingredients in one of the most poignant moments in local sports. A group of World War II veterans, many of them wearing bandages, on crutches and in wheelchairs, came to a spring training game between the Dodgers and Robinson's team, the Triple A Montreal Royals.

About 250 wounded black vets sat in sections which until then had been white only. Anxious city officials chewed their nails and wondered if there would be any reaction from the crowd. There was none.

The black vets who had shed blood for their country stayed put and City Island Ballpark was integrated so peacefully and naturally that no one noticed.

Standing in the shadows, afraid to approach Robinson to ask for an autograph, was a kid from the Cypress Street Midway Section named Ed Charles. He was the victim of many of life's injustices including a broken home, several minor scrapes with police, few goals and no direction.

The charisma of Robinson flooded over the 12 year old.

"I followed him around like he was some god," Charles recalls.

Ed wasn't the most talented athlete on Cypress Street. Heck, friends say he wasn't even the best ballplayer in his family, because many remember the exploits of his older brother, Johnny.

But Charles caught that spark from Jackie Robinson that led him to successful minor- and major-league careers. The glittering testimonial is the World Series ring Ed was worn since he and the Amazin' Mets took the 1969 championship.

The inspiration of Robinson made Ed much more than a dumb jock. Today he's a poet, patriot, coach, role model and friend. In a poem he composed for Robinson's funeral in 1972, he described the major-league trailblazer as *"a spirit aflame."*

Hall of Famer Monte Irvin also has a Daytona Beach connection. His brother Milt Irvin and sister Irene Steward live here, and Monte made a gracious and well-received appearance at City Island Monday night.

Irvin acknowledged that if Robinson had failed he and many others might have been denied their rightful shot at major-league professional baseball. "Jackie was the perfect selection. He was intelligent, aggressive . . . a good speaker. We knew that if he failed, the noble experiment would have been delayed a long time."

Then many in the large crowd were moved to tears by the emotional rendition of "America The Beautiful" by Singer Harry Burney, III. In a curious and wonderful melding of athletics and the arts, the crowd cheered until Burney was forced to acknowledge his feat, much as a slugger is asked to come back out of the dugout after a grand slam.

Robinson, who friends say always treasured and relished his reputation as a pacesetter, would have loved the unveiling of the plaque. Pulling the cloth from the bronze monument were Rufus "Buddy" Young and Freddye Moore, two black commissioners elected to office by citywide vote in this Southern town which is two-thirds white.

Maybe whatever it was about the spirit of Daytona Beach which caught Branch Rickey's attention in the spring of 1946 is still here. Let's hope so.

Monte Irvin summed up the experience for more than a thousand, including a large number of black youngsters, when he exclaimed: "I wouldn't have missed this for the world."

Dick Gregory Didn't Turn out Like Cosby

Who wouldn't want to be Bill Cosby? To say the Coz is one of the best loved men in America is an understatement that beggars description. Maybe he's more trusted than our post-Irangate president or even Walter Cronkite.

Next weekend, area residents will have an opportunity to meet the man who could have filled that Cosby-type niche in the heart of America, but turned it down. If only Dick Gregory could have displayed a lighter sense of humor, or taken his paycheck home and ignored the plight of the less fortunate. . . .

When Gregory burst on the comedy scene in the late Fifties, he was everybody's darling. Yes, there was a biting edge to some of his humor, but it was in tune with the times.

College kids ate it up, bought his albums and memorized parts of his best routines. I was one of them.

Then he purposely ruined it all. The biting edge of humor turned into a buzzsaw. The gently turned phrase became a mirror which told us how ugly and racist our society was — and is.

Dick Gregory started serious protests against the power structure, and his name started showing up more often on police blotters than theater marquees. The public didn't think he was a funny, harmless comic any more.

Whites weren't the only ones who squirmed under the heated Gregory rhetoric. He discomfitted his black brothers and sisters by trotting out statistics on their massive consumption of drugs, liquor, cigarettes and refined sugar.

Instead of one-liners about who was sitting in the back of the bus, Dick Gregory was talking about the lives of stress and poor health care which he deduced amounted to a de facto policy of genocide against poor people around the world.

Not many wanted to listen to that, and some still don't. But Dick Gregory will be in Daytona Beach Saturday night for the finale of the Expo 87 Cultural/Economic Development Fair at Ocean Center.

Sponsors are hoping 500 people (out of the total 5,000 expected to attend the Expo over its two-day run Friday and Saturday) will be attracted by the magic of his name and the power of his message.

The Expo will address a wide range of local issues — some negative, some positive — designed to make this a better community. NFL Football Great Wes Chandler of the San Diego Chargers will lead a "Say No to Drugs" rally.

A respected physician, Dr. Ernie Cook Jr., is a sponsor for the two day event, which includes a Health Fair for several hours both days. Economic development is a prime concern of a second sponsor, County Councilman Big John.

The hard working team behind the scenes is headed by Shirley Rogers and Hugh Grimes of the Central Florida Community Development Corporation.

There is still time to become involved in every facet, but time is short. Reservations for the banquet and Gregory's speech must be made by Wednesday.

A footnote: The booking of Dick Gregory resulted from a chance meeting between the well-known activist and Ms. Rogers at the Atlanta airport about six years ago. "He was such a positive person," she recalls. "a person for the people."

In the '50s, when he made us laugh, Dick Gregory was a leader. He still was in the '60s when he put his life and career on the line for his beliefs. He already was working on world hunger before the rock music community ever figured it out.

Shirley Rogers and I agreed. Today as he always was, Dick Gregory still is a man very much ahead of his time.

Learning More of a Famous Native Son

Writing can illuminate, educate and infuriate. It can help and hurt, sometimes both at the same time. But what's so wonderful about our system of communication is that it can be beautiful. Writing can sparkle and it can shine.

That's why I'm so proud that a native son of Daytona Beach once penned this passage:

"The years, the months, the days, and the hours have flown by my open window. Here and there an incident, a towering moment, a naked memory, an etched countenance, a whisper in the dark, a golden glow — these and much, much more are the woven fabric of the time I have lived. What I have written is but a fleeting intimation of the outside of what one man sees and may tell about the path he walks. No one shares the secret of a life; no one enters the heart of the mystery. There are tell-tale signs that mark the passing of one's appointed days. Always we are on the outside of our story, always we are beggars who seek entrance to the kingdom of our dwelling place. When we are admitted, the price exacted of us is the sealing of the lips. And this is the strangest of all paradoxes of the human experience: We live inside all experience, but we are permitted to bear witness only to the outside. Such is the riddle of life and the story of the passing of our days."

Those were the first words I ever read from the works of Dr. Howard Thurman, and I was hooked. It inspired me to read, almost at one sitting, his autobiography which I checked out from the City Island Library.

Before I had only a vague passing knowledge of Thurman, not much more recognition than his name, that he was born at the turn of the century and that a dedicated group of historians are trying to honor his memory by preserving his boyhood home at 614 Whitehall Street. On an impulse, I decided to deepen my awareness of a person who has brought so much credit to our city.

It's a wonderful story. It contains Howard Thurman's own observations of the strengths and weaknesses of this little southern town. There are heartwarming vignettes of the three black communities of Midway, Newtown and Waycross — all three were Daytona Beach neighborhoods with separate identities and a social structure rich in community loyalty and pride if not wealthy in wordly goods.

Though Thurman occasionally lapses into general descriptions of the area as if he were a sociologist or worse, he is at his best when he produces the telling anecdote, the appropriate example.

It is a story of giving and receiving. Young Howard went from door to door to collect money to bury his father. He painstakingly wrote a letter of introduction to a white business tycoon who lived in a mansion on the "other side" of the Halifax River and won a scholarship of sorts to continue his education. And he counts it a crossroads in his career that an anonymous man once gave him the dollar he needed to check his makeshift luggage at the Daytona Beach train station as he departed to enroll in a Jacksonville high school.

Thurman returned those gifts a thousandfold. He became counselor and confessor to those who were sick and dying. His Howard Thurman Educational Trust has been an open door of opportunity for many years. And he once showed up at a hospital to encourage and uplift an old family friend, Dr. Martin Luther King, Jr., who shortly thereafter embarked on a course of social action which changed our world. It is said that Dr. King often carried a copy of a favorite inspirational book by Thurman in his briefcase during the stormiest years of the civil rights movement. From roots as a kindergarten pupil of Miss Julia Green and attendance at the Mount Bethel Baptist Church here, Thurman blazed a trail which led him to academic honor and worldwide acclaim. He served as dean of Rankin Chapel and professor of thology at Howard University, minister of the interdenominational Fellowship Church in San Francisco, dean of the Marsh Chapel at Boston University and honorary canon of the Cathedral Church of St. John the Divine in New York.

A review of his autobiography in the Atlanta Journal-Constitution describes Thurman as *"one of the great religious leaders of this century."* Vernon Jordan of the Urban League said the story *"should be read by everyone, for in many ways it encompasses the story of all black Americans, a story of barriers to overcome, struggles to succeed in the face of racism, and the development of the inner resources to survive."*

That is true, but I was especially taken with Thurman's insights on my favorite hobby — writing. Deep within the book, one of 19 he wrote, I found a comment on the writing craft which hit me where I live and directly addressed the fine line between true pride of authorship and mere conceit.

It explains why a columnist can be so arrogant as to interrupt your Sunday morning coffee assuming you could care one whit about what he thinks about anything.

Just before his death in 1981, Thurman wrote: *"Again and again I find myself turning to a seminal passage from a book, the words of a poem never memorized. If it is something that I have written, no matter; there is no sense of authorship . . . For this reason I am never embarrassed or surprised when someone speaks of a particular need in him which was met by something that I have written. It is all of a piece, belonging to no one, located nowhere. No one understands the miracle and only the foolishly arrogant dare to lay claim to it as a personal or private possession."*

Festibles & Gatherings

For John, the world was divided into "festivals" — which are festive and fun but an expected part of a year's events — and "festibles" — which are more homemade, with more unusual, even bizzare, touches and are real finds when you happen on them.

"Festivals" enliven a weekend. "Festibles" are recounted in stories for years.

— ML

Festibles' Offer Wealth of Choices for Hungry Patrons

Sufferin' souvlaki and leapin' loukomades!

Is this a wonderful place to live or what? I wish I was five people today so I could be at the Greek Festival, the County Fair, Halifax Art Festival, Pioneer Settlement Jamboree and Skyfest all at one time.

What an embarrassment of riches. So much to do. So little time.

As you might guess, a calendar like today's puts me in that good ole festible spirit. That's in honor of the good folks in Navasota, Texas, I visited a few years back because I spotted their hand-lettered roadside poster advertising a "Blue Grass Festible."

I pulled over and had a great time. Boy, there is nothing like a good festible to promote a positive attitude.

I've been saving a festible roundup and I've been looking for the right moment to use this information.

The roundup includes some stuff on a couple of places I've been to, such as the Black-Eyed-Pea Jamboree in Athens, Texas, and the Breaux Bridge, Louisiana, Crawfish Festival.

In previous columns, I've mentioned the time I went to Athens and watched the judges award the grand prize for the best recipe to the "Pea-tini." It was none other than a dry martini, garnished with a black-eyed pea on a toothpick.

I love to stop in Breaux Bridge, which also hosts a boudin sausage festival and is the home of Mulate's, a great Cajun restaurant. The record for the most crawfish consumed by one person at the crawdad

249

fest is 36 pounds in one hour.

Crystal City, Texas, is the home of an annual spinach festible. This celebration is complete with a spinach queen beauty contest, a spinach bake-off and a parade around the 10-foot tall statue of Popeye the Sailor in the town square.

I'm not making this stuff up. Honest.

Another green veggie with its own festible is the noble zucchini. Each year, Harrisville, New Hampshire, hosts zucchini carving contests, zucchini power-lifting and zucchini look-alike contests.

I've written about pumpkins, so it's no surprise that the orange gourds would have their own festible. It's in Circleville, Ohio, and the highlight is the baking of a 350-pound, 5-foot pumpkin pie.

The health department won't allow the spectators to sample this monstrosity. It is later used as pig food. That's appropriate because the major event in Circleville is a hog-calling competition.

The food tents offer Pumpkin Joes (a lot like Sloppy Joes), pumpkin chips and pumpkin hot dogs.

Recently, the South Carolina metropolis of Irmo, just outside Columbia, had its annual Okra Strut. The big event there is the "Shootout at the OKra Corral" which was won by an Irmo policeman who ate two pounds of boiled okra in only five minutes.

Forget about Pennsylvania the U.S. Senate cafeteria. The real headquarters for bean soup is McClure, Pennsylvania, which has had a festival honoring the beautiful soup since 1891. Legend says it was started by a group of returning Civil War vets and the bean soup was served with hardtack biscuits.

Crackers are now substituted for the hardtack, but the festible roundup article says *"the recipe for the soup is the same — hamburger, beans and lard."*

Utica, Illinois, lays claim to the title of Burgoo Capital of the World. It's a game and vegetable stew which is simmered in large kettles for at least 15 hours.

One of the recipes used in Utica calls for 600 pounds of red meat, 200 pounds of chicken, 2,000 pounds of potatoes and a whole bunch of other fixin's.

I close with a mention of the Gilroy Garlic Festival. This California town is famous for its garlic flavored treats, such as pasta con pesto, scampi and calamari.

For dessert, you can get a heaping bowl of garlic ice cream.

One booth hawks garlic corsages, which might come in handy in vampire country, and a fragrance called Garlique. The slogan for the garlic perfume is: "He may forget your name, but he'll know you've been there."

The garlic fields of Gilroy are so famous that they attracted the notice of the noted humorist, Will Rogers, his own se'f.

Will drawled that Gilroy is "the only town in America where you can marinate a steak by hanging it on the clothesline."

Toadmaster Title May Be Just a Leapfrog away

All regular column readers know that Toad Suck Daze has always been high on my list of "festibles" even though I've never actually had the pleasure of attending one. It's already too late for this year's because it was held May 5-7. I have a year to plot my strategy for the next one.

But merely showing up isn't enough for me. My goal is to someday attain the lofty rank of (gasp!) Toadmaster. Woody Cummins is the current Toadmaster and is unlikely to relinquish the title anytime soon.

It's the biggest honor in Conway, you understand, and I hear that you've got to be plugged in to Arkansas politics, public service and charity to be considered. Doggone it, Woody. I WANT THAT TITLE!!!

Just to give you an idea of the neat things Toadmasters get to do, they hug beauty queens and hobnob with big-time politicians like President Bill Clinton and Governor Jim Guy Tucker. The festival got mentioned by Jay Leno on national teevee this year.

I've been sent a whole bunch of Toad Suck Daze clippings from the hometown paper, the Log Cabin Democrat, including a special Sunday supplement pullout section of the paper with lists of events, features and Toad Suck related advertising.

It had messages like *"Frigidaire employees wishes all you Toads and Toadettes a Toad Tappin' good time." "Get toadally fit in the relaxed atmosphere of an all-women's gym and spa."* I also noticed an ad which commanded, *"Look what's hoppin' at Payton Greek Catfish House"* and a real estate ad by Michelle Parsley warning: *"Don't live under a toadstool. Try one of Parsley's Picks."*

My favorite was the one for Eve's Intimate Apparel, which said: *"Hop on over to our lily pad . . . you will croak over our toadal bargains."*

The special section also had a brief article of self-praise. *"The toads aren't the only things croaking with joy. The Toad Suck Daze Committee has a little something of its own to croak about this year."*

Turns out that the Conway group earned honors at this year's meeting of the Arkansas Festival Association. Toad Suck Daze was second only to the Hope Watermelon Festival (which, strangely enough, I actually attended when I was a little jug-eared kid) as the state's "Festival of the Year."

I've gone all this way without telling some of you new readers the story about how the Toad Suck festival got its name. Seems that back in the days when steamboats plied the Arkansas River they would tie up at Conway to drop or load cargo or to bide time when the water was too low to travel safely.

The crewmen on these boats were considered riffraff by some of the townsfolk. And the rough river types lived up to the stereotype by drinking corn squeezin', cussing and fighting at the little lean-to tavern on the riverbank.

Legend has it that a little church lady complained about the riffraff by sniffing: "They sit down thar suckin' on moonshine jugs 'till they swole up like TOADS!"

That story may not be true, but by golly it ought to be.

The only things fresh squeezed in Conway these days are the lemonade and the beauty queens. The event is famous for crawfish, funnel cake, homemade potato chips and chicken on a stick.

The only thing Conway doesn't have, and needs desperately, is a Toadmaster the likes of me. I think that would be toadally awesome.

Carter's Valentine Cupboard Full of Helpful Hints

Vice President Al Gore should never quit his day job and try for a career as a stand-up comic.

He has acquired a rep for being somewhat wooden and humorless.

That may not be true, because I found a line I really like that was said by Gore when asked his opinion of that unusual institution called the vice presidency.

He cracked: "I feel like Zsa Zsa Gabor's fifth husband. I know what I'm supposed to do, but I don't know if I can make it interesting."

That pretty much sums up our challenge today, boys and girls.

It is Valentine's Day, and you may choose to view this as a rote obligation or a challenge to make it interesting."

It's funny that I would even dare give advice to the lovelorn. Everyone in my family has been married so many times that they're throwing Minute Rice at our weddings.

When it comes to affairs of the heart, I'm a rebel without a clue.

Here are the main items in Carter's "Cupid" Cupboard:

1. If you haven't bought your loved one a nice Valentine's card and gift by the time you are reading this, it is already too late.

Go ahead and scramble for a gift anyway . . . it will suffice for minor damage control . . . but don't be fooled by outward indications of forgiveness.

You will pay, and you will pay for the rest of your life.

2. Do not heed any requests from your loved one not to bother with

an expensive gift.

Be wary of advice from so-called experts that you can do something cheap but intensely personal, like create a homemade "credit card" for kisses, hugs or tasks from the job jar and get away with it.

Little kids can get away with homemade cute Valentines.

Grown-ups can't. Simple as that.

3. Don't be too sophisticated. Do not dismiss romantic notions because they are too corny.

Be old-fashioned. Remember that in the Victorian era folks swooned a lot. Swooning is good. Plan to swoon at the drop of a hat.

Remember that Victorians got a bad reputation for their attitudes about sex, but history shows they actually were having sex all the time, those tricky rascals.

I think swooning was the key. I plan to swoon a lot and you should, too.

In the inimitable words of Cole Porter, *"Birds do it, bees do it."* And that is actually the historical essence of Valentine's Day.

During the Middle Ages in England and France, it was associated with folklore that birds began to pair up and mate halfway through the second month of the year.

Chaucer mentions this:

"For this was sent on Seynt Valentyne's day, When ever foul cometh ther to choose his mate."

That ole Chaucer is a famous writer, but looks like he couldn't spell a lick.

By the way, historians say there were three Saint Valentines, but facts about them are a bit scarce.

The one I like the best is the priest killed by Emperor Claudius Gothicus because he disobeyed the rule against performing marriages for Roman soldiers.

Claudius wanted his soldiers to be lean, mean fighting machines unencumbered by family ties.

Saint Valentine secretly married soldiers and their brides until he got caught and was executed.

I've been flippant about Valentine's Day so far, and that's bad.

If I don't end on a serious and romantic note, I'll likely pay for it the rest of my life.

So here is my vote for the most romantic Valentine's story of all:

Charles, the Duke of Orleans, was taken prisoner at the battle of Agincourt in 1415, and was kept in the Tower of London for 25 years.

He penned more than 60 Valentines, the first written examples of that form. They are on exhibit at the British Museum.

Here is one of the beautiful messages to his French lady love:

"Wilt thou be mine? dear Love, reply
Sweetly consent or else deny.
Whisper softly, none shall know,
Wilt thou be mine, Love? aye or no?
Spite of Fortune, we may be
Happy by one word from thee.
Life flies swiftly ere it go
Wilt thou be mine, Love? aye or no?"

Crawfish Festible Delightful for Momma's Boy

Happy Momma's Day, y'all. As you read this, I am down in Hollywood lavishing gifts on my own dear sainted mother and I hope y'all are doing likewise.

It hasn't been easy being my Mom, and I think she has done it about as well as anyone could. Look at it this way, Mom, what if I had been twins?

I rest my case.

After all the sonly duties, I may leave early to check out the Cajun-Zydeco Crawfish Festival in Fort Lauderdale. Y'all know how much I love "festibles," and I especially love the ethnic cuisine types.

You may call them crayfish and I say crawfish, but my friends and relatives in the corruptocracy of Louisiana call the li'l fellers "Mud-bugs." I am uniquely qualified to talk on this topic 'cause I have on occasion set mudbug traps in a Slidell, Louisiana, ditch and caught my own, then boiled them up with po-tatoes and ears of corn.

The lowly crawfish is not only associated with dingy, stagnant water, it is a staple of most Texas, Louisiana and Mississippi political rallies, which are even more dingy and stagnant.

Some snobs put down mudbugs, calling them derogatory names like "Swamp Things" and even worse "Ditch Food."

Crawfish deserve better however. They actually are a close relative of the lobster and they are mentioned prominently in that gourmet bible, the Larousse Gastronomique.

257

I always like to quote from Larousse because I know how much y'all love it when I speak French. Anyhow, crawfish are tres bien as all get out and are called "ecrevisses" in high-toned cookbooks.

Though "Ecrevisses Cardinal" has been an appetizer on the menu at Antoine's Restaurant in New Orleans for 150 years, mudbugs haven't been a big restaurant or festival hit until recently.

Crawfish are actually nutritious and a good source of protein. One book even listed them as an aphrodisiac. I dunno about that. I ate a dozen of them one time and only one of them worked.

The reason crawfish have come to mind is that the gentleman who is providing mudbugs down in Lauderdale is planning to come to Daytona Beach.

Promoter Lee Webb has invited the crawfish king to bring his huge infernal mudbug boiling machine to Main Street for a little demonstration. This experiment has the blessing of some Main Street merchants and will go before the Main Street Redevelopment Design Review Board. I got a little tickled at Lee's request to the city for the event, which was submitted mainly as a courtesy 'cause almost all of the festival will be on private property. Lee was a good sport about it, mainly because he thinks festivals ought to be fun and, like P.T. Barnum, believes there is no such thing as bad publicity.

Lee has gingerly referred to his event as a "mini-festival" which won't attract a large crowd and is "a test event to introduce people to crawfish".

Lee said that isn't literally true and that he has faith that folks hereabouts are gonna love crawfish, but he laughed when I told him it was the first event ever promoted in this town that wasn't glowingly described as colossal and the greatest thing since sliced bread.

This idea of a "test festival" intrigues me no end. Does that mean we'll hear loudspeaker announcements on Main Street saying: "ATTENTION! This is a test. This is ONLY a test. If this had been an actual crawfish festival, you would have been having fun!" or "Kids! Do NOT try this at home!"

"For the next three minutes, we will sound the tone for a test of the southeastern crawfish festival network. Do not adjust your sets."

Well, Lee told me I could have my little laugh now, but it'll all change, and, Lee says he may be telling me about the colossal, crowd-magnet, hot time, Main Street crawfish festival and he'll get the last laugh.

You could be right, Lee. If that happens, just consider this a test column. If it had been a real column, I would be paid more.

Let the bon temps roll!

Oooooh, Aaaaah,
Fireworks Tonight!

Thank goodness we got some rain recently so we could celebrate this wonderful anniversary of our independence with fireworks. There is something about the loud and colorful aerial displays that brings out the kid in all of us.

Oooooh . . .

Ka-POW!!! . . . pop-pop-pop-pop

Aaaaah . . .

Breathes there a soul so dead that a Fourth of July fireworks show cannot stir it to thoughts of patriotism, motherhood and apple pie?

The late Herbert M. Davidson, who edited and published this newspaper when I was hired almost 23 years ago, once told me his idea of the perfect newspaper headline: a two-word banner headline that would tell a story and cause hearts to leap in gladness.

HMD said those can't-miss words were "FIREWORKS TONIGHT!"

Well, in his honor, those words ring out again today and this evening, as we celebrate all that is good about our republic.

The history of fireworks is muddled a bit, but there is general agreement that the Chinese invented them in the second century B.C. to frighten evil spirits and celebrate weddings, eclipses of the moon and victories in battle.

They also had some undefined religious purpose and the underlying science behind fireworks evolved into "flaming arrows" of warfare.

The military applications were quickly seized by Islamic cultures in the Middle East. An Arabian writer named Abd Allah made the first written reference to "Chinese snow" in the 13th century.

It's believed that the Arab improvements in gunpowder were then reintroduced into China and became the basis for rocket science. European crusaders were fascinated by them, again mainly for military uses, and took knowledge of their manufacture home.

Berthold Schwarz, the legendary "powder monk" of Frieberg, is the center of a legend that he invented black powder and set the stage for modern warfare and modern fireworks shows.

But it was a group of Italian artisans who soon became the undisputed masters of the art and many of their descendants make up important fireworks manufacturing families even to this day.

It wasn't long before immigrants brought fireworks to America, where they were an instant and enduring success.

The only negative was that mischievous pranksters in the Rhode Island colony misused the dangerous combustibles and in 1731 brought the very first ban on their use in the New World.

So you see, controversy over fireworks is nothing new.

On July 3, 1776, John Adams wrote a letter to his wife explaining the actions of the Continental Congress and speaking of the desire to sever ties with England. He suggested that independence be celebrated with *"much pomp and with illuminations,"* or fireworks.

It wasn't long before politicians made good use of the shows during campaigns and by 1892, a fantastic aerial show at the Brooklyn Bridge was witnessed by a crowd estimated at 1 million souls.

New York also was the site of what is believed to be one of the greatest fireworks shows ever staged. Three famous families in the business: Zambelli, Grucci and Souza, put aside their competitiveness and worked together on a show marking the 100th birthday of the Statue of Liberty. It was July 4, 1986.

This show used 22,000 aerial bombs, launched from 30 barges and other vantage points. An additional 18,000 set pieces, ground pictures, fountains and low displays stretched from the East River to the tip of Manhattan, along the Hudson River, around Miss Liberty and Ellis Island.

The production required 220 miles of wire, 777,000 pounds of mortar tubes and a staff of 100 pyrotechnicians. And what is so funny, kids watching that display probably were disappointed when it ended and whined to mommy and daddy that they wanted to see more.

As you can see, the American love of fireworks runs pretty deep. I've said in closing so many of the columns in the past: "Too much ain't enough."

A family gathering at Lake Okeechobee — John, daughters Karen and Ginger, nephew Jeremy Bailer and son David.

How Did Jack End up with that Lantern?

Now, once upon a time, there was a fellow named Jack. He was not a nice guy.

I hope that my Irish-American readers are not offended at this stereotype, but Jack was a boisterous, brawling son of the Emerald Isle who lost many bouts with demon alcohol.

He got so drunk one night, October 31 to be exact, that he was near death.

The Devil, that sly deceiver, arrived to snatch his soul, but Jack was not ready to cash it in yet, and like a true Irishman, he began to bargain with Old Scratch.

The legend gets a little long here, but suffice it to say that Jack outwitted the Devil (it's funny how stupid Satan is in Irish folklore) and escaped with his life and soul intact.

In fact, at one point Jack persuaded the Devil to leave him alone for eternity.

But that move backfired. Jack's wasteful ways finally caught up with him and he went on to what he hoped was his great reward.

However, he was rejected for entry into the Pearly Gates because he had been too evil, and even more amazing, the Devil said a deal was a deal and Jack wasn't welcome in Hell.

This trapped Jack in a sort of limbo, and as he trudged off in the dark, the Devil threw him a glowing lump of brimstone to light his way. Jack hollowed out a turnip and put the glowing ember in it and

263

used it to light his path.

And that, dear readers, is one version of the story about how the Jack O'Lantern became part of All Hallows Eve, or Halloween.

The devil made me do it. I couldn't resist capitalizing on the fact that today is Halloween, even though some of you probably celebrated it Saturday because tonight is a "school night" for the kiddies.

Though the Irish used turnips and beets as lanterns, we use the pumpkin as our Jack O'Lantern veggie of choice.

Many historians blame the Irish for the whole doggoned holiday. It is, they say, derived from a Celtic festival called "Samhain," or "end of summer." It celebrated the beginning of winter and the Celtic New Feast of the Sun.

It was a signal for families to store as many provisions as possible for the hard winter ahead. The Irish also believed that it was the day of the year that the demarcation between the living and the dead was the thinnest, and dead souls roamed the land.

The Irish are also credited with beginning Trick or Treat. Peasants would go door to door begging for money or food in preparation for festivals. Also it was considered good luck for neighbors to give and receive gifts.

In other parts of Europe, the faithful baked "soul cakes," which were freely given to anyone who came to the door during the festival. This also is thought to be a precursor of the Trick of Treat tradition.

Many years later, this festival attracted attention from the Vatican, which substituted All Saints Day to replace the pagan festival. Pope Gregory III was the one who moved the observance to November 1.

The Irish started it, but the Scots named it. Young people still celebrate the Scottish Hallowe'en by building bonfires on hilltops and then they dance around the flames. The custom is called Hallowe'en bleeze.

In America, immigrants from Ireland and Great Britain brought the tradition with them. Irish families fleeing the Great Potato Famine settled in New England, where they taught everyone the charming custom of tipping over outhouses and unhinging fence gates on Halloween.

Jack Santino, author of "Halloween and other Festivals of Death and

Life," wrote that the holiday has a special status in our lives because it arose from the experience of the people, and was not forced upon us by higher authority.

"Halloween has become one of the most important and widely celebrated festivals on the contemporary American calendar, and it is not even officially a holiday," he wrote. *"No day off is given for Halloween, no federal decree is proclaimed establishing it as a national holiday.*

"People simply do it."

265

Daydreaming of a White Thanksgiving

Thursday was Thanksgiving and there is much to be thankful for this year. If all goes as planned, I will be romping in the snow with my two grandsons as you read this.

The whole family is holed up in a condo in Silver Creek, up near the Rocky Mountain National Park and very close to the town of Fraser, which ought to be called "Freezer" because many days it reports the coldest temps in the Lower 48.

I'm returning to Colorado for a visit after many years. I'll be very interested in what the place looks like these days. I may not like it.

I got hooked on skiing back then, and may get up the gumption to try it again this week, that is, if there is enough snow. At the time I left, it wasn't a sure thing there would be enough white stuff to support skiing, snowboarding, sledding and other wintry pursuits.

Gobble, gobble! OK, you've got a lot of leftover turkey in the fridge and you aren't really sure what to do with it.

That can only mean that it's time for me to repeat my recipe for the world's "most perfect turkey sammich."

Anyone who remembers their childhood knows very well that sammiches are much better than mere sandwiches, and here is proof. There's no reason why leftovers can't be just as good or better than the original article.

First, find some really good bread. Fresh-baked sourdough is one of my favorites, but excellent fresh bread is one of the keys to this comestible.

Then slather a goodly amount of mayonnaise on both sides. I hate dry sammiches.

Take some leftover turkey and stack it. Then top it with the crispest, prettiest lettuce you can find, crisp lettuce being another key to snack nirvana.

Here's the neat part. Top THAT with cranberry sauce, jellied or berry, it doesn't matter, and garnish THAT with chopped walnuts.

Now there's a leftover treat to be thankful for.

What Did You Forget this Christmas

By now, we'll all know if we done good this year, picking out presents and wrapping them with care. But there are some things that you forgot. Don't ask me how I know. I just know.

For instance. That Magical-Morphological Pomegranate Ranger you bought for the kids requires four AAA batteries. You either didn't remember to buy any batteries or, if you did, you bought either only two AAA batteries or four AA batteries.

You also forgot your promise never to buy an unassembled bicycle again. You were up until 3 a.m. putting this one together and you were short three parts, but ended up with two parts left over.

One of the pedals is hanging forlornly at a 45 degree angle because you stripped the threads before learning the thing went on counter-clockwise, not clockwise.

The instructions, of course, were printed in Taiwanese.

You are now trying to call your mother-in-law on the phone to wish her a happy holiday. All circuits are busy.

You busted the family budget to buy your little tyke all the prestige toys known to Madison Avenue. You shelled out big bucks and melted your charge card in the quest for the Little Miss Cuteness doll or the Transmorgrifier of the Cosmos Interplanetary Disco.

The toys are sitting on the floor next to the piles of wrapping paper while your kid plays with the vacuum cleaner.

In spite of all that, the human spirit reigns, and Christmas comes shining through as a happy time. When I was just a little jug-eared kid growing up in Jacksonville, Christmas was for me a time for a new basketball, that first baseman's mitt I had been begging for and a new chemistry set, because I had used up all the chemicals which would explode in my old one.

I hardly ever got yucky ole clothes, and the holiday season was filled with new toys, games and pieces of sporting equipment. In return, I gave my grandparents, who raised me, pretty much the same thing each year. They didn't care and loved me anyway.

I would buy my grandmother scarves or handkerchiefs and I would get after-shave or shaving soap mugs for my granddad. He kept a row of bottles of after-shave and men's cologne on his dresser, all testaments of past Christmases, birthdays and Father's Days.

The older bottles were only about half-full, not because he ever used them, but because of evaporation. I guess he loved me a lot. He never threw them away and they always were proudly on display.

The fun places to be at our house during the Yule holiday were the kitchen and the dining room. We had a large cedar buffet in the dining room that had many drawers festooned with ornate brass handles.

In the bottom two drawers and behind side doors were holiday fruitcakes, banana-nut breads, rum cakes, bourbon balls, almond cookies and Swedish wedding cookies all wrapped in towels.

Most of the fruitcakes were soaked in orange juice, but my very Baptist grandmother would bathe a couple of the fragrant cakes in whiskey. It was one of the few vices she allowed in the house, and then only because it was her idea.

These were the good kind of fruitcake, not the bad kind that had lots of, Ugh!, citron peel. My grandma made her cakes with lots of pecan pieces direct from the heart of papershell pecan country in South Georgia. The main glaced fruits in the cakes were cherries and pineapple.

Usually a couple of the cakes had nothing but pecans and cherries, and I think I liked those the best. My grandma used to pretend to get mad at me when I would eat a piece of her spiked fruitcake, slice o' rum cake or a bourbon ball and then swerve around the room acting like I was drunk.

I told her someday they would find me in the gutter with crumbs on my face.

Lots of company would come on Christmas Day. The kids would meet out on the front porch to tell each other what we got and decide who came out best, while the adults gathered around the dining room table to sip hot cider and cinnamon, drink eggnog and graze lazy susans full of fruitcake, bourbon balls and cookies.

The menfolk would furtively move to the back steps, where they would pet my cocker spaniel Rusty, smoke cigars and pour booze from a flask into their eggnog cups. The women, good Baptists all, pretended they didn't know what the menfolk were doing.

This year, I'll be celebrating Christmas out in Arlington, Texas, with my young'uns David, Karen and Ginger and my grandson Conner. We won't have to hide the hootch inside cakes or sneak flasks out in the back yard. But I know some things won't change.

I prob'ly got the wrong size batteries for Conner's toys and about now we'll look up and find him playing with the vacuum cleaner.

Merry Crispness, y'all!

Confessions of a
Klutzy Packager

I could save a little money each year on those little "To . . . From . . . " tags you put on Christmas presents. No one ever has to look at the tag to identify gifts I put under the tree.

Just look for the crooked, wrinkled paper with the ripped corners and the big bulge of paper loosely tucked in one side and about to break the bonds of 16 small pieces of Scotch tape. Yep. That one's from me.

I've really tried, but never got the hang of wrapping presents. And everyone else can. I believe I'm the only person in the whole world who can't wrap presents with crisp, neat corners and a smooth unwrinkled surface.

It would be enough to scar a weaker person, or one who doesn't have many other serious faults to worry about. It's one of those things I've resigned myself to, like:

I'll never win the Florida Lottery.

I'll never be awarded an honorary doctorate from Harvard.

I'll never earn the Nobel Prize for physics.

I'll never win the Daytona 500.

I'll never understand Holly Hill politics.

And, I'll never acquire the basic motor skills it takes to wrap a socially acceptable package.

Hey, my standards aren't high. I'd like to be able to wrap a passable package, instead of those misshapen lumps that cause smirks and condescending comments.

How would you feel if your uncle held up a package you had labored over for more than an hour with eyebrows knitted and your tongue stuck out of the corner of your mouth and declared: "Looka here. I know who did this one, Haw Haw Haw! Hey Johnny, what's inside here? A toaster oven or a dead possum?"

Even my kids, who love me and have faithfully believed all the many lies I've told them over the years without complaining, roll their eyes when they see the pitiful packaging of their Yule gifts. I think this one issue alone has been a main contributor to the lack of respect I receive.

My own dear sainted mother, who tells me I am the light of her life, smiles that smile that mothers smile. Even my mother once teased me by joking: "I want to open this carefully so I don't mess up the wrapping."

I know those of you who can whip out a hospital corner in a jiff or tie a perfect bow in a nanosecond have no idea what I'm talking about. You've never wrapped a mile with my shears.

And in your lack of understanding, you will make such cruel and off-the-mark comments like "So what? Every department store and shopping center has hundreds of ladies and even some men who can wrap a package so tight you can bounce a quarter off it. Shell out a little money, tightwad, and spiff up those packages!"

I've done that, of course. And on Christmas Day when the presents are handed out, my relatives make cutting remarks. "Oh look. John had somebody else do his gift wrap this year." "Oh look how pretty this package is, and you did it ALL yourself, didn't you John" . . . (wink) (wink) (smirk). "I think this package is mislabeled. It says it's from Johnny but it can't be, not with the way it's wrapped."

If Daytona Beach Community College, Stetson, Bethune-Cookman or even Embry-Riddle would offer a night vocational training course in how to wrap Christmas gifts, I would consider it. Do they award scholarships to the culturally deprived? Is there any way to overcome lack of motor skills? Will I ever find the tag end of the Scotch tape now that it has disappeared into a dispenser and is invisible on the roll?

You may think this is trivial, but it applies to other life skills. It explains somewhat why I am also so bad at making beds, tying shoelaces and setting tables.

Anyhow, enjoy your Christmas Eve and the big day itself. And if there is one present shoved over in the corner that looks like it was dropped off a 10-story building or used as a soccer ball, then think about me and how I wished you the happiest holiday ever.

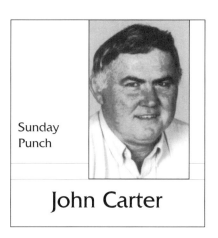

Sunday
Punch

John Carter

John Carter died behind the wheel of his pickup truck in the Florida countryside, June 20, 2000, at the age of 60.

He is missed.

Contributors

"The Jug-eared Kid" would not have been possible without:

Tippen Davidson, Publisher of The News-Journal, who had the idea in the first place.

John's family, Dot Reese, his mother, and his daughter Karen. They generously shared their photographs and memories.

Dru Jones, Promotion Manager of The News-Journal, who with her staff, researched and produced copies of the 700-plus columns from which "The Jug-eared Kid" was taken.

Mark Lane, long-time pal of John Carter's, who assisted in selecting the columns used. He was a constant support in the daily evolution of the book.

Tom Lindley, Toni Picha, and Linda Klayman of the NJ Creative Services Department, who had type set and produced a readable book design without ever being out of sorts.

Steve McLachlin, former Art Director of the newspaper, whose witty and insightful drawings enliven both the book and its cover.

Jim Tiller, head of The News-Journal Photo Department, who edited and reproduced all of the photographic material.

And finally . . . Doug Spence, Commercial Printing Manager, who somehow, got the book out on time.

Martha Van Camp
Editor